Grow your own
WEDDING
FLOWERS

Grow your own
WEDDING
FLOWERS

How to grow and arrange your own
flowers for all special occasions

GEORGIE NEWBERY

Published by

Green Books
An imprint of UIT Cambridge Ltd
www.greenbooks.co.uk

PO Box 145, Cambridge CB4 1GQ, England
+44 (0)1223 302 041

First published in 2016, in England

Georgie Newbery has asserted her moral rights under the
Copyright, Designs and Patents Act 1988.

Illustrations © 2016 Fabrizio Boccha
Front cover photograph © Georgie Newbery
All interior photographs are by the author, with the exception of the following.
Page 81: © Howell Jones Photography. Page 152: © Heather Edwards.
Pages 160-1 & 184: © Sim Canetty-Clarke. Page 215: © Sarah Mason.

Design by Jayne Jones

ISBN: 978-0-85784-253-4 (hardback)
ISBN: 978-0-85784-258-9 (ePub)
ISBN: 978-0-85784-265-7 (pdf)
Also available for Kindle

10 9 8 7 6 5 4 3 2 1

CONTENTS

To my parents, Gilly and Nigel Newbery

Gilly, the gardener and florist, who taught me that if you just get on
and do something then you'll get much further than if you first sit about
wondering if it's possible or not.

Nigel, the thinker, who is still trying to teach me that if I think while I do,
then I can be strategically ready for barriers I will inevitably hit if I've not
prepared for them in advance.

Acknowledgements

Writing a book while running a business is a triumph of the desire to write over
common sense and time constraints. Because I take centre stage where the
press, and therefore credits, for Common Farm Flowers is concerned, publicity-
wary Fabrizio is sometimes sidelined. And yet, without his support and encourage-
ment, it would not be possible for me to snatch my writing time from family
breakfasts and happy Sundays. (I write this while he has taken the kids off to see
Sweet Track, the Neolithic road across the Somerset Levels, and I have the house
to myself: fire lit, Bach playing, kitchen table mine alone.) His is the common-
sense practicality grounding my flights of floral fancy. Without his digging, compost
moving, mulching, rabbit-proofing, fencing, gating, mowing and doing most of the
cooking, Common Farm Flowers and my flower-related books would not exist.

The rest of the Common Farm Flowers team too deserve all my thanks: Sharon,
Emily, Ann, Phil, Nic and Karen.

And thanks to Alethea and Jayne, the editor and designer of this book, who turn
my cursive chat into something that is both a reference resource and the inspiration to others that I intend it to be.

FOREWORD

As a gardener who has grown cut flowers for 20 years, I can totally see why many of us love the idea of growing all the flowers for our own weddings. It's hugely satisfying – from seed to bunch or flower crown – and you'll have a cut-flower patch humming with bees in the meantime. Then there's the scent of real garden flowers and the twist and turn of a stem, which you rarely get in flowers commercially grown; not to mention the small fortune you can save by growing and arranging your own.

It's possible to do and I hugely recommend it, but it's worth having some advice and expertise to set you on the right track. It's good to know how many flowers you'll need and how to get them ready on the right day: how to cut, condition and arrange them. That's exactly what this good and useful book will tell you. Georgie has kept it simple – the gardening information given in an easy-to-digest, matter-of-fact way; the cutting and conditioning advice really useful for someone who might be an experienced gardener but might not have spent much time cutting their plants for posies or bouquets. How much space do you need to grow a wedding? How many stems do you need for wedding flowers? How long do they need to condition before being used in floristry? That's all here.

Georgie describes herself as a gardener rather than a horticulturalist, and her floristry is all self-taught. If she can grow flowers for over 50 weddings a year, then her advice and experience is just what will help you to grow your own successfully for your wedding day.

Sarah Raven
www.sarahraven.com

INTRODUCTION

Imagine a wedding, and what do you see? A bride and groom; happy, smiling faces . . . and flowers. I'll bet the third thing you think of when you picture a wedding is the flowers. Flowers frame a wedding, enclosing the happy couple in a bower of loveliness. I've never heard of a wedding that didn't have at least a bouquet for the bride and a buttonhole for the groom. Flowers are in almost every photograph of a wedding – dressing the people, the ceremony, the aisle, the tables, even the lavatories! What would a wedding be without flowers?

Yet wedding flowers can be enormously expensive. And rightly so. Ask a florist to arrange even just a bride's bouquet, three bridesmaids' posies, five buttonholes, and (for a small wedding) perhaps three table centrepieces, and that florist will probably be up at 6am creating the most immaculate and exquisite arrangements. Good florists know how important the flowers are to a bride and groom, and go to great lengths to make sure that wedding flowers are the most beautiful confections they make. The roses must be just right – open, but not going over; the trailing honeysuckle exquisite; the bride's bouquet so lovely the florist can hardly bear to give it away. So, yes, even for a small wedding scheme, flowers created by a professional florist should be expensive.

But wedding flowers aren't just financially pricey. Couples are becoming more concerned about the environmental cost of their nuptials. They don't want their happy celebrations to be filled with flowers doused in chemicals and flown in from far, far away. They want their wedding day to be beautiful, but not at an unsustainable cost to the environment.

So more and more couples are looking for locally grown flowers. And those with gardens, time, inclination, helpful relatives . . . might be looking to grow those flowers themselves. After all, back in the day, the grannies did all the wedding

Opposite: A bride's hand-tied bouquet with garden roses for an early-summer wedding.

Jam-jar posies can be stunning in a wedding scheme.

flowers, with blooms grown by the grandads. For my wedding my mother wandered my late-autumn garden and put together a bouquet of one nerine lily, old man's beard, blackberries, purple dogwood leaves, acorns and oak leaves. It cost nothing but a little of her kind time, and a stretch of ribbon to tie it all.

This book is designed to be a practical guide to growing and arranging wedding flowers for yourself, whatever season you plan to hold your wedding in. It will show you how to plan, grow, cut, condition and arrange the flowers for your wedding – from table centrepieces to a beautiful hand-tied bride's bouquet.

Whether your aim is just to keep your flower budget under control, or your dream is to grow your whole wedding scheme, this is the book for the home-growing bride and groom: the couple who don't want their wedding to cost the earth.

How to use this book

First there's the gardening, but there's also the planning for cutting, conditioning and arranging your flowers. How many stems will you need? How much space to grow them? Where should you put your flowers when you've cut them? I've aimed to cover all this in these pages. The point of this book is that you should feel confident, when it comes to the days before your wedding, that the flowers you've grown can be cut, conditioned and turned into arrangements, in plenty of time, without any last-minute adrenaline rushes.

I've tried to ensure that the book is presented in a way that makes it easy for you to use. Yes, there are plenty of photographs, which should provide inspiration for what you might do with the flowers you grow, as well as what you might grow.

I also appreciate that weddings take place throughout the year, and so I've split the wedding planning section into seasons, so you don't have to read a lot about late-summer planting if you've booked to be married in spring.

I've also included a section with how-tos for those who are planning their floristry. If, having read these sections, you feel you'd like more detailed practical help, then I do recommend a day's course with a florist teaching wedding floristry for people planning on doing their own.

A note on quantities

For some of you, the idea of a hundred guests may seem onerous; for others, too few, but in this book I cater (floristically) for a wedding designed around a hundred guests sitting at ten tables, with both sets of parents, three bridesmaids, a best man and one usher (groomsman). Bear that in mind when making your own calculations, and you can scale up or down depending on the numbers you plan to involve at your own celebrations.

A note on seasons

I hope that couples in countries around the world will read this book and be inspired to grow their own flowers, and so, rather than referring to the months of the year by name, I've used generic translations ('early spring', 'mid spring', etc.). I expect that people planning to grow their own wedding flowers will already have a good idea of the timing of the seasons in their own garden, and so I leave readers to gauge for themselves when their 'early spring' or 'high summer' may be, wherever they live. If your climate is colder than average, you will have a shorter flowering season, with a later spring and an earlier autumn than in warmer climes, so bear this in mind when you plan your flower growing. (For example, in the far north of the UK, 'early spring' may not come until April, whereas in the warmer south-west it will be March.)

By the way, I use 'midsummer' to refer to the month of the summer solstice; 'midwinter' to the month of the winter solstice (June and December respectively, in the northern hemisphere). To refer to the middle of the summer growing season (July in the northern hemisphere), I use the terms 'middle of summer' or 'high summer', while 'mid winter' refers to the middle of the winter season (January in the northern hemisphere).

To put the advice in this book in context: in the south-west of the UK, where we grow our flowers, the climate is broadly equivalent in temperature and season to zone 9 in the US system of plant hardiness zones.

The higher the sun in the sky and the longer the days, the wider the range of flowers and foliage one can grow to cut. However romantic and candlelit a winter wedding may be, the options for home-grown flowers and foliage at that time of year are fewer. However, I still say that a winter wedding can be just as magical as a summer one – with candles, and greenery, and perhaps the bride in a hooded velvet cloak . . . Whatever the season, the sowing and growing lists in this book are there to inspire you: snapshots, if you like, of the myriad varieties available to grow. Take my ideas as a starting point, and continue your research by trawling the lovely seed catalogues available online.

Horticultural Latin

Throughout this book I've tried to refer to plants in a way that will be most useful to you, the reader. If the plant is generally known by its Latin name (or an anglicized version of its Latin name), then that's what I've used, but in most cases I've used the common name by which a plant is generally known in the UK. Please see Appendix 1 for the Latin and common names for all the plants described in this book. I'm conscious that plants may be known as something quite different in, for example, the USA. This is why horticultural Latin is such a useful tool for gardeners!

Who will be growing the flowers?

Forgive me if in these pages I speak often of the bride as the decision-maker, thereby apparently excluding others. Of course, a wedding is a day for a *couple* to plan, with their friends and families involved, and a wedding day is not exclusively the bride's to dictate. However, if I constantly said "The couple, and their parents, and . . .", etc. at the beginning of any sentence suggesting one action or another, this book would be unreadable. Indeed, it is often the mother or mother-in-law-to-be of the bride who grows the wedding flowers, while the father or father-in-law-to-be provides a little muscle in the flowerbed-prepping area. Sometimes it is the groom who is more interested than the bride in the flowers. I do try to ring the changes a little when I talk about who is in charge of decisions, so as not to sound as though it is always the bride who decides everything from day one of an engagement.

Who are we?

The 'we' I talk about throughout this book are me, Fabrizio – my husband and business partner – and the team at Common Farm Flowers in Somerset, south-west England. We began a business growing cut flowers to be used in our own floristry 5 years ago almost to the day (as I write this on 31st March 2015, the business is 5 years old tomorrow). We now cater to around 50 weddings a year, as well as sending flowers by post throughout the UK mainland all year round, and teaching a great many workshops – including how to grow your own wedding flowers, and how to arrange your own wedding flowers. Since we started Common Farm Flowers, the 'slow flowers' movement has really taken off, with growers around the world beginning to offer a locally grown alternative to the hundreds of millions of very samey flowers supplied by multinationals, who grow in vast tracts of land around Lake Naivasha in Kenya, on mountainsides in Venezuela and Colombia, in parts of northern India, etc. Slow flower growers often have the health of the environment at the heart of their business ethos, seeing what they do as an opportunity to feed the bees as well as to grow beautiful, scented, fresh flowers to sell to their locale for a living. We are proud to count ourselves as just such a business.

The author installing an arch of flowers for a country wedding in Somerset.

PART ONE
PRACTICAL MATTERS

CHAPTER ONE

PLANNING AHEAD

So the decision is made. You are going to be married. The next question is, of course, "When?" It's rare that I come across couples who are married in 6 weeks (as I was). Most people have 6 months to a year of planning time. And 6 months will give you plenty of time to plan if you'd like to grow your own wedding flowers.

Why grow your own wedding flowers?

There are several reasons why you might wish to take this route. The obvious ones are: a) cost; b) a love of gardening; c) an exciting challenge.

Cost

At the time of writing, couples in the UK can expect to spend, on average, somewhere in the region of £1,500 to £2,000 on flowers for their wedding. The flower budget alone can hit the £20-£30,000 mark if the scheme is to be seriously luxurious, involve a lot of fiddly floristry and require a large team to transport and install the flowers (as well as take them away) at a weekend.

You may understandably wish to save some of this cost: after all, a few packets of seed will cost you very little. That said, the *time* required to grow your own flowers is a different kind of commitment, which it's worth considering before you decide on the grow-your-own approach.

You love gardening

If you, or members of your family, love gardening, and already have a good, established garden you can cut from, this is the ideal situation. When the Duke and Duchess of Cambridge were married in Westminster Abbey in 2011, a great many of the flowers that festooned that enormous old church were cut from royal gardens. You might not have that kind of acreage to cut from – but then you are probably looking at a more

A jug of foxglove 'Sutton's Apricot', an easy-to-grow biennial found proliferating in many gardens, makes a great addition where there's room for a tall arrangement.

manageable guest list of around 100 rather than several thousand, and therefore a smaller venue to dress with flowers. A well-established garden of mixed perennials and shrubs, with a few annuals put in especially, should be able to supply plenty of material for a home-grown wedding.

You love a challenge

Maybe you just want to have a go at it, on a piece of land you've spied! You can grow plenty of cut flowers for a wedding in a space perhaps half the size of your average

A cornucopia of garden flowers cut fresh from beds you planted yourself is a great reward for all your hard work in the garden.

A mix of flowers in jugs and jars makes for a very pretty wedding. This is a late-spring combination with roses, sweet Williams, ox-eye daisies, buttercups, fox-and-cubs, orlaya, ammi majus, nigella and clary sage. About half of these were grown from seed, but the rest were cut opportunistically from established beds and our wildflower meadow.

A bride's bouquet doesn't have to be whites or pastels. Here a riot of late-spring colour, bursting with foraged wildflowers as well as those cut from the garden, makes a gorgeous bride's posy.

allotment. So, even if you have no garden to cut from at the outset, don't be put off: with the necessary space, a strong back, careful planning, growing your own should be perfectly possible.

How much to grow

In this book I will tell you how to grow enough flowers for the following:

- a bride's bouquet
- three bridesmaids' posies
- five buttonholes
- one large arrangement for the church
- ten table-centre posies
- three large, jug-sized arrangements for the reception.

If you bear this in mind when you think about how many arrangements you'd like, you can scale the quantities given here up or down, according to your requirements.

Stem-counting

This is the boring part, but if from day one you know roughly how many stems you'll need, then you can work backwards to plan your planting. The following ball-park numbers give an idea of what you'll need per arrangement.

- Jam-jar posies: 20 stems – so for 10 table-centre posies you'll need 200 stems.
- Large jugs of flowers: 50 stems – so for 3 jugs you'll need 150.
- Pedestal arrangement: at least 75 stems.
- Bride's bouquet: takes more than you might think – about 50 stems.
- Bridesmaids' posies: each will take about 35 stems, so for 3 you'll need 105 stems.
- Buttonholes – we use a minimum of 5 short stems each, so for 5 buttonholes you'll need 25 stems.

And there you have it – a whole wedding in 605 stems!

Now, 605 stems might sound like a lot, but remember that about a third of those can be foliage (in the winter that proportion may be greater; indeed, you may make the whole wedding scheme out of foliage) – so then you only need grow 405 stems for your wedding flowers. You could plant just 500 of the same tulips, or 500 narcissi, and there you have your wedding – all the single-flowering plants can be planted to flower on time (weather permitting) especially for your day. And 500 tulips or narcissi planted shoulder

A big bucketful of flowers will make a large jug arrangement and the bride's bouquet (left and centre), plus a few small posies.

In winter, handfuls of foliage and berries, such as this mix of variegated pittosporum and wild spindle berries, could make a solid basis for your whole wedding scheme.

to shoulder could take as little space as one 3m by 1m (10' x 3') bed. Not too much space, nor too costly, when you think that you can buy tulip bulbs for as little as £10 for a net of 50 bulbs. So there you go: your budget is suddenly set to £100 for your whole wedding flower order. Admittedly there is the cost to your back and the space in your garden, and a teeny amount of stress about whether they'll be in flower on the right day – putting all your eggs in one basket is a little risky – and you have to cut, condition and arrange them. But the main point is that if you take your flower-growing plans and split them into discrete projects like this, then what you have to do to achieve your home-grown wedding becomes really quite manageable.

What to plant

Your choice of flowers will of course depend on the season you have in mind for your wedding. You might even want to schedule your wedding to fit the time of year when your favourite flowers are in bloom. Whether it be spring for tulips, early summer for roses, autumn for sunflowers, late winter for white anemones smiling through a mass of flowering ivy in a tiny, country church . . . We will look at specific seasons in later chapters. Use this chapter to make your initial plan.

Be sensible about what will be possible at any given time of year. You can't expect annuals that start flowering in late spring to be in tip-top condition to cut for an autumn wedding, for example.

To get you started, in the table below are some easy lists of cut flowers, foliage and filler, and some wildflowers that you might be able to find. These lists are by no means definitive: they're just to give you inspiration and help you begin to make your plan.

Knapweed cuts beautifully into wedding flowers. You might find butterflies visiting your reception if you use these in your scheme.

IDEAS FOR FLOWER COMBINATIONS				
	Spring	**Summer**	**Autumn**	**Winter**
Cultivated flowers	Narcissi	Sweet peas	Sunflowers	Anemones
	Tulips	Roses	Japanese anemones	Ranunculus
	Peonies	Cornflowers	Dahlias	Hyacinths
	Irises	Ammi majus	Ammi visnaga	Narcissi
	Grape hyacinths	Delphiniums	Cosmos	Amaryllis
Foliage & filler	Early emerging leaves	Bupleurum	Bells of Ireland	Flowering ivy
	Cow parsley	Alchemilla	Bronze fennel	Holly
	Fruit-tree blossom	Mint & other herbs	Sea holly	Euphorbias
	Sun spurge	Garden shrubs	Mint & other herbs	Willow & dogwood
Wildflowers	Cowslips	Buttercups	Wild carrot	Blackthorn (sloe) berries
	Bluebells	Ox-eye daisies	Wild scabious	Old man's beard
	Snake's head fritillaries	Sorrel	Knapweed	Spindle berries

Don't forget the neighbours

You are not the only gardener in your vicinity. Your neighbours' gardens may have good supplies of ivy, roses and other goodies. I have two lovely clients who each have a daughter being married from home next summer, their ceremonies 6 weeks apart. These two ladies live near one another and both have well-stocked gardens, and they're planning to grow a good selection of annuals to supplement the perennials and foliage they already have to hand. They are working together; both gardens supplying both weddings – a great plan!

Obviously you need to *ask* the neighbours if you can have a nice chunk of that flowering ivy, or some of their lovely roses. I don't want to be accused of encouraging larceny! But gardeners are usually generous sorts, and neighbours often neighbourly, and the chances are that they won't mind being asked. They may even, if you ask them far enough in advance, offer to grow something for you. Is there a kind gentleman down the lane who always wins prizes at the village show with his sweet peas? People love to help, especially with a wedding.

A word on style

Please indulge me while I say a few words on style.

Wedding flowers don't have to look 'weddingy'. In fact, one of the great advantages of growing your own and arranging them yourself is that you can ensure that your flowers will be full of life and dance for you. The chances are that you won't have the skills required to make your flowers into a solid mass of lifeless constraint, which is what I often see when I look at 'designer' wedding flowers.

So take this opportunity to think cleverly about colour: just because you're growing wedding flowers doesn't mean you must automatically think pink. If the garden where you're to hold your reception has a stunning custard-yellow 'Graham Thomas' rose growing around the door, then think about yellow. Yellow, white and green make such a fresh combination.

Think about dark colours too: choose interest over 'bridal', and go with the seasons. The people whose gardens you may beg extra

Some gardeners can't help but grow too many sweet peas and will be happy to let you have some of their surplus for your wedding.

'Graham Thomas' is a gorgeous yellow rose, full of scent. Here it's in a posy with ammi majus and white Jacob's ladder.

with the colours easily available to you, because growing your own is great, but it would be churlish to turn down a garden of roses to pick just because they don't go with your childhood dream of pale pink for your wedding.

When to plant

So the plan is made, you know roughly how many guests and therefore how many table-centre posies you'll need, you know the venue, you know how many brides-maids and ushers, you know the date . . . But don't start planting yet!

Work backwards from your date and sow or plant accordingly. The following is a guide-line, for every season through the year. And when it comes to annuals, always hedge your bets: the key to success is successional sowing. Remember to sow little and often, and all will be well.

material from won't have planted a scheme with your wedding in mind, but will have created a garden that goes with the seasons as they unfold. Spring gardens are generally made up of pinks and purples, with some blues. Midsummer gets pinker and whiter, with also dark red and yellow roses. And as the season goes on the colours heat up, with jewel-coloured dahlias, sunflowers, fiery heleniums – taking you through until the first frosts. It might be wise to work

❀ For a mid-spring wedding, with tulips and narcissi and early wildflowers, you'll need to plant most of what you need through the autumn of the previous year: specifically, narcissi and daffodils in early autumn and tulips in late autumn. Spring wildflowers such as cowslips can be grown on from a sowing the previous summer, to make good-sized plugs which can be planted out in autumn for flower-ing in the spring.

Just because you're growing wedding flowers doesn't mean you must automatically think pink.

A jug of sweet Williams in late spring, grown from seed sown early the previous summer.

- For a late-spring wedding you may choose to have a scheme involving biennials sown the previous summer, and possibly the first annuals, sown direct or under cover the previous early autumn. Don't forget lovely perennial peonies, which may be in flower in your or your neighbour's garden. If you decide to be married in the spring but are too late to sow biennial or perennial seed to have

your own plants ready in time, garden centres and nurseries often have good chunks of seedlings for planting out in the autumn. Wallflowers, for example, can be bought bare-root, often just wrapped in damp newspaper, in quantities of 20 or 50.

- For an early-summer wedding you'll probably want to use roses, along with the first annuals. Sow annuals in both autumn and spring, to hedge your bets against the vagaries of the weather.

- For a wedding in the middle of summer, annuals sown that year – either in seed trays under cover in late winter, or direct into warming ground in early spring – should be beginning to flower.

- Late-summer weddings can be tough: early-sown annuals are likely to be going over, and, depending on the summer you're having, you may find that the seed you've sown at the beginning of the season has sprouted, grown, flowered, gone over and is already no good to you. So, as ever with annuals, successional sowing can be the key to success.

- For early-autumn weddings, annuals should be sown no earlier than mid spring, and for a good crop in early autumn I recommend perhaps fortnightly sowings of small amounts of seed right up until early summer. As I write, it is coming on to mid autumn, and in the

Work backwards from your date and plant or sow seed accordingly. When it comes to annuals, the key to success is successional sowing. Remember to sow little and often.

WHY DO WE HAVE FLOWERS AT WEDDINGS?

It may be that originally they were to conceal the background smell. The world in the old days was a stinkier place: the air a miasma of undrained sewage and unwashed people. Flowers would have had to work hard to fight that, but at least the bride would have had a posy to dip her nose into for some relief.

People who have ears of corn in their wedding flowers are nodding to ancient fertility rights, though they may not know it!

polytunnel we have zinnias and sunflowers in full flower, which I didn't sow until midsummer this year.

- Mid-autumn weddings will use the last of the perennial garden: final-fling roses, dahlias (so long as you've been deadheading them since they started flowering, as early as the middle of summer) and foliage turning to autumn colours. But annuals sown in early summer will flower until the first frosts, so it's worth planning to have a few in reserve, especially if you have some cover (a polytunnel perhaps) to grow them on in. Again, as I write, in mid autumn, I have a fresh crop of self-seeded annuals in my small tunnel just beginning to flower – a welcome mix of cornflowers and ammi majus, which are giving my arrangements a lovely light feel to balance the richness of the autumn colours.
- Going into winter, you'll need a great deal more foliage and perhaps forced bulbs for flowers – paperwhite narcissi, hyacinths, amaryllis – perhaps all grown under cover. Evergreen shrubs will help here, especially variegated varieties.

Choosing and buying seed

When it comes to deciding exactly what to grow, it pays to spend some time looking at all the options. Sit down and take a few hours to trawl through seed suppliers' websites or mail-order catalogues.

Why order seed direct from the supplier? Well, it will be fresher and will have been kept in optimum conditions (cool, dark, dry), whereas seed sold by garden centres is often kept for months at a time in conditions similar to a hot greenhouse, and might not be as fresh as it could be.

Furthermore, seed suppliers will give you a much wider choice than if buying from a garden centre, where the options will be limited by space and by what the managers think customers are likely to want to grow.

Making your choice

You're better off with, say, five or seven varieties of flowers than with just a few each of

An easy-to-grow flower such as cosmos (this variety is 'Purity') can be used as a fallback in case of failures.

many more. Keeping your choices down will give your wedding flowers a 'look', not too matching, but you'll have enough of each variety that your scheme will look designed rather than random.

Do keep your colour palette in mind. This sounds very obvious, but it's easy to get excited when buying seeds and end up with an assorted mix of black-striped sweet peas, blue cornflowers, orange pot marigolds,

yellow annual chrysanthemums – which is all very well if that's your choice, but when growing your own you have the opportunity to grow to a colour scheme. So do think about the scheme you would like, and keep to it: for example, blue, yellow and white; or pastels; or hot jewel colours. Perhaps make a 'mood board' to put all the pictures of the flowers you like together – whether sticking the pictures of the flowers you like into a scrapbook, or using an online tool such as

If you decide to be married in the spring but are too late to sow biennial or perennial seed to have your own plants ready in time, garden centres and nurseries often have good chunks of seedlings for planting out in the autumn. Wallflowers, for example, can be bought bare-root, often just wrapped in damp newspaper, in quantities of 20 or 50.

Pinterest. Then you can check not only whether they'll flower together at the same time, but also whether they look lovely as an ensemble.

Choose one or two flowers that will make more of a statement in your arrangements. For spring, you might choose tulips; in early summer, roses; in high summer or early autumn, perhaps sunflowers or dahlias. Florists call these 'accent' flowers. You don't necessarily need loads of them. In a jam-jar posy, just one big dahlia head framed by a handful of cheery annuals can make a finished arrangement. If each of your jam-jar posies has one strong accent flower head, then your arrangements will look very pleasing to the eye, even if they're spread over quite a large reception area.

In addition to accent flowers, other shapes can help to make your bouquets and posies dance: spikes, daisy shapes, lace caps and buttons. You should also choose one flower that is easy to grow and can be massed effectively: sweet peas, cosmos or ammi majus, for example – these can be your fall-back in case of emergency. Lots of cosmos in a jug is gorgeous to look at, as is a big bunch of sweet peas. If all else fails, you'll have these blooms to rely on.

Top tips when starting out

- Be sensible about what will be flowering at the time of year your wedding will be. Sticking pictures of peonies in a scrapbook when you're planning an autumn wedding won't make peonies flower for you then.

- Make a mood board of the flowers you'd like to have in your scheme. This way you can make sure you've got a nice mix of colour, textures and shapes.

- Aim for about five to seven types of flower, plus other goodies – perennials, foliage and wildflowers – that you can find in season.

- Don't forget plants that are already established and will be in flower at the right time in other gardens. Does Granny grow that gorgeous rose you love? Ask people to help, and you'll save yourself time and give yourself more choice.

- Order seed direct from seed companies: it'll be much fresher and give better germination rates than seed that may have been languishing in a hot garden centre's shop. And a good wholesaler will be able to give helpful advice on varieties, flowering times, and even mixtures that will look good together.

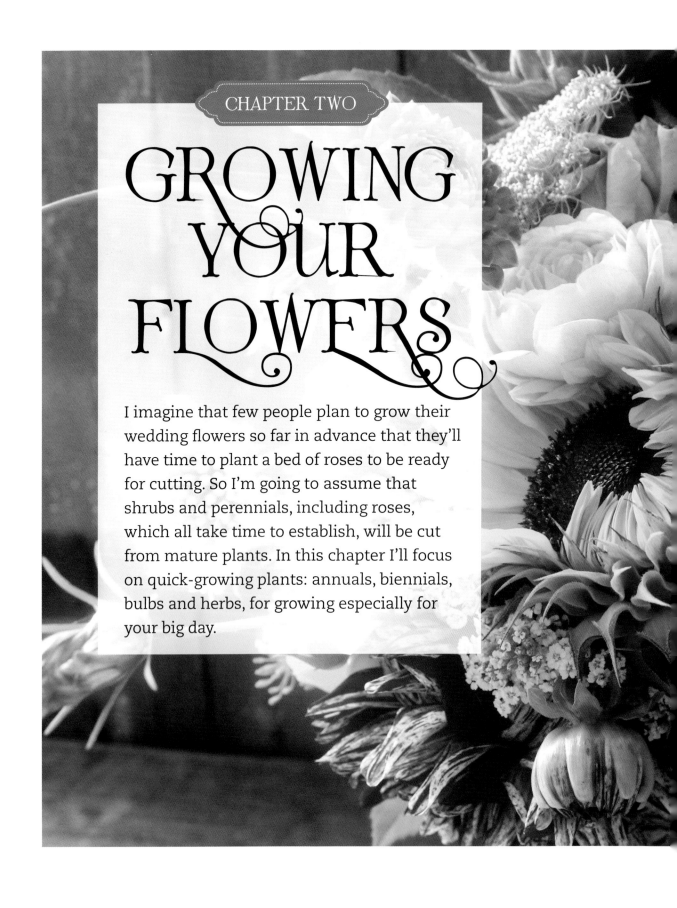

CHAPTER TWO

GROWING YOUR FLOWERS

I imagine that few people plan to grow their wedding flowers so far in advance that they'll have time to plant a bed of roses to be ready for cutting. So I'm going to assume that shrubs and perennials, including roses, which all take time to establish, will be cut from mature plants. In this chapter I'll focus on quick-growing plants: annuals, biennials, bulbs and herbs, for growing especially for your big day.

Your flower patch will be a beautiful thing to enjoy in itself, as well as supplying flowers for your wedding.

This bed, weeded and raked to a fine tilth, is 1m (3') wide and 3.5m (12') long. Three times as much as this should be plenty of space in which to grow your wedding flowers.

Ground preparation

As with all gardening, the health of the earth in which you grow will determine the success of your crop. So prepare your ground carefully. Before you plant anything, the ground needs to be clear of weeds, fed, and raked to a fine tilth. Take the time to pull out roots of perennial weeds. If your ground is dry and well drained, add moisture-retaining compost. If it's clay and tends to hold too much water in wet weather, dig in grit to help with drainage. Compost will also help to break up clay soil.

To get the best possible performance from your flowers, you should feed not only the plants but also the soil. So before planting, add garden compost and/or well-rotted manure. Here at Common Farm Flowers, we feed our soil with a mix of horse manure and compost tea. Recipes for making plant- and soil-feeding teas can be found on page 39. (For a more in-depth look at growing cut flowers, I refer you to my previous book, *The Flower Farmer's Year*, but this book is intended to supply you with lovely blooms for your wedding, not to put you off with too much detail before you've even begun!)

A warning note about horse manure

Horses are often fed on hay from fields which have been treated with weedkiller, to suppress docks in particular. This goes straight through the horses, comes out in their manure and takes years to break down. If you put this kind of manure, even very well rotted, on your garden as a feed you risk seeing your plants come up twisted, stunted, yellowy and generally unhappy. So for your precious garden, use only manure from horses grass-fed in fields that you know have not been sprayed with weedkiller. This is easy enough to do in the summer months, when horses are put out to graze.

Avoid using manure from horses that have been fed on bought-in hay, because the owners of the horses won't be able to reassure you without doubt that the hay is uncontaminated.

A row of nigella seedlings in midwinter. Sown direct into the soil in the autumn, they'll need thinning out to a 22cm (9") spacing in early spring if the plants are to grow large and give lots of nice, long-stemmed flowers.

For details about planting bulbs for cutting, see Chapter 4.

Sowing seed

Once you have clean (weed-free) soil that will rake nicely to a fine tilth, then you can sow seed direct into the ground (a good idea with hardy annuals, which you can sow in the autumn; or for a late-summer wedding, for which you can direct-sow into warm ground in spring). Alternatively, start your seeds off in seed trays to germinate under cover, such as in a cold greenhouse. For an early-summer wedding, you might get them going under cover in autumn or late winter, to be planted out as good-sized seedlings in spring (see Chapter 5, page 94).

Direct sowing is great if you have space, once the soil is warm enough, but of course your seedlings will be more vulnerable to pest damage. I recommend hedging your bets by sowing a tray of seed as well for every variety you sow direct – this way, if your strip of healthy cornflower seedlings are eaten off one night by a marauding army of evil slugs, you'll have back-up.

Don't be tempted to direct-sow too early: test the soil warmth by holding your hand flat a few inches above the soil during early spring. You'll feel nothing but cold and

I recommend hedging your bets by sowing a tray of seed as well for every variety you sow direct.

nothing but cold and nothing but cold – and then, bingo! One day you'll feel the warmth radiating from the ground. Time to start sowing!

Spacing

For sowing seed directly into the ground, make your rows about 22cm (9") apart, and when the seedlings need thinning, thin them to 22cm apart too. This may seem space-greedy when you have a tiny row of seedlings, but you want those seedlings to grow into large, floriferous plants, and they won't do so well as they might if they're fighting for space above ground, and their roots are crowding for water below. If they have to share little water, you might find your plants get mildew, which, while it won't kill your flowers, doesn't make for beautiful foliage in your bride's bouquet.

If raising your seeds in trays, sow them thinly into free-draining, peat-free seed compost. We make our own seed compost by mixing two-thirds municipal green-waste compost (with the chunky bits picked out) with one-third sand. This makes a good, serviceable seed compost, and is a great deal less expensive than using bought preparations that are specifically labelled for seeds. When seedlings are big enough to prick out, separate them into module trays, one seedling per module. A seedling is big enough to prick out once it has a good pair of leaves, by which you should handle it – never by its stem, which can bruise easily when the plant is this tiny. Once you see the

Seed-sowing parties are great fun. The more help you have with your flower growing, the less stressful it will be – and what are bridesmaids and ushers for if not to be put to work?!

first curl of a root peeking out of the hole at the bottom of the module tray, potted-on seedlings are ready to harden off and plant out (see page 37, 'Summer management').

When and how much to sow

If you think you'll need, say, ten plants per variety of flower you want to grow, to be in full flower for your wedding, then if you have a space like the bed shown in the photograph on page 32 (right), you could easily fit two rows each of, say, five varieties of cut flowers across the bed.

You need to hedge your bets a little with timings, because a hot spring will have your flowers going over more quickly than a cold, late spring – and, no matter where you live, you can never predict the weather in advance. The way to avoid being caught out by the vicissitudes of the weather is to sow successionally. So, in a second, similarly sized bed, you could fit the same number of plants again, sown 2 or 3 weeks later, and in a third bed you could have the same yet again, sown another 2 or 3 weeks later. For tulips and spring flowers, you can be clever and plant some of your crop in pots, which you can then bring in to force if necessary.

Autumn-sown hardy annuals will flower from late spring / early summer onwards. If your wedding is booked for early summer, then you might like to direct-sow one crop of your chosen flowers in the autumn, but also put in another crop, either under cover in late winter or directly in the ground once the soil's begun warming up in spring. If you have mild winters, your

Consider including herbs

If you're planting a bed of a size like the one pictured on page 32, you could edge it with pineapple mint and lavender; with thyme and rosemary. Herbs are lovely in posies – the scent of mint mixed with sweet peas and roses has to be one of my absolute favourites; a sprig of rosemary makes a cheerful upright in a buttonhole, and can also be used in memory of a much-loved family member who may no longer be there. Lavender can be very calming to a nervous bride. If the lavender goes over, cut it anyway and save it to scatter on paths to and from the ceremony or on the way to the reception. You'll likely get a second flush of flowers, and with the dried lavender scattered on the ground, people will wonder where the wonderful scent is coming from.

Mint works very well in posies – here with the gentle bobbing blue heads of campanula.

autumn-sown plants will be flowering for you (so long as the slugs didn't get them all) early next summer. But who knows what the winter will do? Sow more seed in trays in late winter, and it will fill any gaps in your overwintered stock (see Chapter 5).

Pests

Outdoors, there are slugs and birds and rabbits, which might take your seedlings. Birds can be frightened off with bits of something glittery hanging above your beds: old CDs or strips of silver foil work well. Slugs can be deterred by ringing your plants with coffee grounds (easily available from your local coffee shop if you don't produce enough from your own kitchen) or smashed, baked eggshells (bake off the membrane inside, which might otherwise attract rats). Rabbits can be fenced out.

Even if you raise your seedlings in trays under cover, the risk of pest damage is ever-present, so do take precautions:

- **Slugs** A salted smear of Vaseline around the lip of a seed tray makes double protection from the dreaded slug. Of course, if you move any of your seed trays, or disturb them, you risk smudging off this smear, so make sure to reapply your salty Vaseline.
- **Mice** The only seed I *never* direct-sow is sweet peas, because the mice will have it in a heartbeat. Always sow sweet-pea seed in deep pots of good, free-draining compost and cover with a mouse-proof, clear lid until the seed is well germinated. Mice will dig over all your seedlings once they've found germinating

sweet peas, just in case everything else is as delicious – so it's worth taking care!

- **Greenfly** As the weather warms in spring, you may suddenly find you have an infestation of greenfly on your precious seedlings before you've had a chance to plant them out. You can squeeze them off between finger and thumb, but you risk damaging easily bruised growing tips that way. Another option is to spray greenfly with a very weak soft-soap solution (a short squirt of washing-up liquid in water in a sprayer bottle). Don't spray soap solution on plants when the sun is full on them, or you risk scorching the leaves, so this is a job for a cool evening or early morning.

I always start sweet peas off in trays, and only plant them out when they're about this big, for fear of marauding mice eating the fat, sweet, germinating seeds.

DID WEDDINGS ALWAYS HAPPEN IN CHURCH?

Actually, no. Historically, weddings would take place in the porch of a church. Marriages were legally binding contracts between families, and the church porch was a good, large, dry place for people to meet. Only 1,500 years after the beginning of Christianity did marriage become a sacrament to be celebrated at the altar of a church.

Overwintered seedlings

If you're growing for a spring or early-summer wedding and have trays of autumn-sown hardy seedlings in a cold greenhouse or cold frame, you may occasionally find that they're frozen solid in a hard frost.

Help them survive by preventing them from defrosting too quickly: make a tent of sacking or burlap to wrap them up, and they will defrost slowly and stand a much better chance. Don't worry if they appear very frost-bitten: the frost is simply pinching out the growing tips, as you might yourself later in the year, and they will have lots of flowering shoots ready to surprise you in the spring.

If you have seedlings sown in beds to over-winter outside, and the conditions are freezing, you can either cover the beds with fleece before the frost to protect them, or cover with green mesh, burlap or sacking after the frost, to prevent too-speedy defrosting. I will admit to being quite lazy, and unless there's been a period of really warm weather in which my seedlings have

suddenly put on a bit of sappy growth, I don't protect them. Only in spring, if there's a late frost, do I worry, and then I fleece them so long as I know the frost is coming.

Summer management

Surviving winter is one thing; growing in the garden through the summer is quite another. Don't take your eye off the ball, and keep in mind the following points.

Don't let seedlings growing in trays dry out. Water them from underneath, to help prevent the possibility of mould on the surface, which might cause damping off (when seedlings collapse and rot, ruining your plans), and check regularly that the water is getting all the way up through the compost. If the leaves of good-sized seedlings look a little yellow, you can feed them with a very weak seaweed solution to give them the trace elements they might need.

Remember to harden off seedlings for a good fortnight before planting them out. 'Hardening off' means putting seedlings midway between the warm, protected environment they're used to and the cold of the open garden. You might harden them off outside but against a wall somewhere, or in an open cold frame if you have one.

When you plant out seedlings into the ground, water them in really well – if necessary watering the bed before you plant the seedlings into it, watering the seedling in the pot before you take it out of the pot, and watering again once the seedlings have been planted. From then on, don't water more than once a week, in order to allow the plants to get their roots down and find water deep in the soil.

Sweet peas can be especially prone to mildew. Plant them a good 22cm (9") apart and be prepared to water and feed them for really high-quality flowers. We never expect a sweet-pea plant to be in full productive flower for more than 6 weeks at a time, so don't sow too early.

Seeds growing in the garden where they've been direct-sown shouldn't need so much watering. At Common Farm, we water in seed when it's sown – as much to tamp down the earth around the seed, so that emerging roots won't hit air pockets, as to give the seed moisture to encourage germination. Once the seeds have germinated, unless it's very dry, you shouldn't need to water much: maybe once a week during a dry period, but probably less often than that. However, if your plants are looking at all mildewy, give them a good water. Mildew is often caused by dry roots.

Feeding

There are lots of reasons for feeding your plants: to encourage strong growth, to encourage lots of flowering shoots, to keep leaves green and healthy, and to help plants fight mildew and botrytis (mould), as well as slug and aphid attack. At Common Farm, we feed our plants with a mix of nettle tea, comfrey tea, chicken-poo pellets and seaweed solution. Recipes for garden-feeding teas are given opposite, but if you don't fancy making these, then a good supply of organic chicken-poo pellets and seaweed solution are the ingredients I recommend.

As mentioned earlier in this chapter, for best results you should feed both the plants *and* the soil. As well as adding garden compost and/or well-rotted manure (see page 32), you can also feed your soil with compost tea.

When planting seedlings out, add a scattering of rockdust (which comes from the sides of volcanoes) dusted into the hole you're going to plant into. Like seaweed solution,

Home-made garden-feeding teas

Nettle tea recipe In the spring, once the stinging nettles are shooting, cut a good quantity of them and put them in a bin. Fill the bin with water, cover, and leave for 3 weeks. The resulting stinking soup makes marvellous, nitrogen-rich plant food. Dilute 1:10 (or weaker) with water, and feed your plants fortnightly with it to promote strong growth. Use until midsummer.

Comfrey tea recipe This is a potassium-rich preparation, which will help your plants be extra-flowery for your big day. In the middle of summer, cut the whole of a comfrey plant off at the base (don't worry, it will regrow). Chop it up a little and put it in a bin. Cover with water and a lid and leave for 3 weeks. The resulting mess smells even worse than nettle tea, but diluted 1:10 it makes a wonderful once-a-week feed for mid- to late-summer flowering plants. Remember: feed your plants with this stinky tea no closer to your wedding than a week. You don't want your flowers to smell of comfrey juice!

Compost tea recipe In a washing-up bowl, put a handful of well-rotted manure, a handful of garden compost (not sterile, shop-bought compost), and a handful of freshly shooting nettle tips. Fill the bowl with water and put it somewhere in full sun in a warm place, like a sunny greenhouse. Stir from time to time over 48 hours, and you'll see a bubble of yellow scum forming on the surface. This is a wonderful bacteria tea, breeding in the mix. After 48 hours, dilute 1:10 and use to feed the soil you'll be planting into. Use this to make sure your earth is in extra-good heart before planting.

this provides a mix rich in trace elements, which will help plants to establish.

Until midsummer (when the days are lightest), feed freshly planted-out seedlings with a nitrogen-rich food such as nettle tea, to encourage long, strong stems. However, if using commercially prepared feed, do read the instructions carefully: strong concentrates can burn your seedlings, while much-watered-down concentrates will feed them.

Feed the plants you plan to cut from for your wedding fortnightly from when they start flowering with a very weak seaweed solution: this is full of trace elements and rich in potassium, which will help make lots of flowers. It should also help fight mildew and prevent yellowing leaves. Or, if you'd like to make more of your own free plant food, feed fortnightly with comfrey tea, which is also potassium-rich. At Common Farm, we feed with both comfrey tea and seaweed solution, alternately through the high-summer and late-summer months. Your time may be precious and your comfrey supplies meagre. Seaweed solution works very well if you don't have comfrey.

If your plants are looking at all mildewy, give them a good water. Mildew is often caused by dry roots.

Cut a bed of dahlias for a wedding on a Thursday, and the plants will be in full flower again by Saturday, which is great if you plan to hold your reception in the garden where you grow your flowers.

Weeding

I did warn you that growing your own wedding flowers would take a little bit of time, and one of the jobs it's worth spending time on is weeding. For the same reasons that you don't want overcrowded plants, with roots fighting each other for limited water supply – because the plants may become mildewy – you don't want your plants to fight with weeds for water, space and light.

If you plant your seeds or seedlings in rows 22cm (9") apart, then you can easily run a hoe between them once a week or so, and this will keep your soil clean and give your plants lots of space.

Staking

If you're growing annuals for a summer wedding, then you'll need to think about plant supports. All this care and attention,

These dahlias are growing through netting pulled taut horizontally across the bed, protecting them from summer wind and rainstorms.

feeding them and giving them lots of space, means that your plants will be tall, and a strong wind might flatten them if you're not careful.

You may be growing flowers in various empty spaces in the garden, in which case each little clump of plants will need to be supported with canes. If, however, you're growing your wedding flowers all together, in an allotment-style patch or part of your vegetable garden, then your plant support can be easier to manage.

Sweet peas will do better grown in a straight row up pea netting rather than up a tepee-style arrangement of stakes. Why? Well, sweet peas growing up a tepee will jungle in the middle of the structure, and it'll be really difficult for you to find all the flowers to cut them and thereby make sure the plants don't go over before the big day. Sweet peas grown in a line along pea netting are very easy to keep tied in and the flowers cut.

Other annuals, if grown all together, can be netted with pea netting *horizontally* across the bed. Plant four stout stakes at the corners of your bed, and perhaps two more halfway along the bed, if it's long. Then hook the net-ting over the stakes, pulling it down to a height of about 1m (3'). Alternatively, make a cat's cradle of string criss-crossing over the bed. Do this before the plants are too tall (it's much easier to stake plants *before* they are tall enough to need it), and they'll grow up and through the netting or string, enjoying the support.

You can use this trick with dahlias and roses too, if you're growing them in a block.

Top growing tips

- 🌸 Always water trays of seedlings from underneath, to avoid damping off.

- 🌸 Sow the same mix of flowers two or three times over 3-week intervals: that way you won't be caught out by unexpectedly hot or cold weather, bringing your flowers to bloom too early or too late.

- 🌸 Plant out or thin your seedlings to 22cm (9") apart. This way their roots won't fight for nutrients or moisture, and you won't find your flowers suffering from mildew because their roots are dry.

- 🌸 Feed your plants with a nitrogen-rich feed until the midsummer, and a potassium-rich feed thereafter. You can make your own plant-feeding teas, or use a very weak seaweed solution for a good all-round fortnightly feed.

- 🌸 Water well, but not too often. Water in plants really well when planting them out, and perhaps once a week after that, but not more often. Plants that are watered too often have very shallow roots, which not only means they will suffer in a dry period, but also that they will struggle to stay upright in a strong wind.

CHAPTER THREE

CUTTING AND CONDITIONING

I think the easy part of doing your own wedding flowers is the growing. I know I've given you quite a detailed chapter on the process of sowing seed and managing seedlings, but really, as you very likely already know, raising flowers from seed is mostly a matter of sowing seed, watering it, and then watching the flowers grow.

It's probably the cutting and conditioning of flowers that people worry about more than growing – and rightly so! Approach cutting with a devil-may-care attitude, and you risk disaster. Cut your flowers carefully and condition them properly, and you'll have the best-quality, beautifully scented, gorgeous flowers for your wedding.

For best results

In fact, cutting and conditioning flowers is no dark art: it's really a matter of good practice. Follow the guidelines below, and all will be well.

When to cut Early in the morning, or in the evening. If you can feel the heat of the sun on the back of your neck, then don't expect flowers to survive being cut.

How to cut With clean, sharp scissors. Use carbon-bladed florist's scissors rather than secateurs (unless you are cutting thick, woody stems). You'll quickly give yourself repetitive strain injury if cutting over 600 stems with secateurs. Cut at a sharp angle: this gives the cut part of the stem maximum surface area for accessing water, through the exposed sponge-action cellulose cells.

As you cut each stem, strip the foliage so that the stems go into the buckets clean.

For a wedding, cut flowers when they are half to three-quarters open. If it's warm weather, a fully open rose cut on a Thursday will have gone over by Saturday. Cut them part open, and the stress of being cut, then getting an unexpected drink, and being moved to a warm place (which your reception venue

Styling tip

Setting out the reception tables

Make sure the tablecloths are unfolded and laid so that the ironing creases point the same way throughout the room. This gives a pleasing tidiness on which your delightful table decorations will be the centre of interest. Equally, if you have runners going across or down the length of tables, it's more effective if they all go the same way.

For a simple but effective way to add detail to your 'tablescapes', add a sprig of lavender or rosemary to the place name cards.

Write names on simple brown card labels and add a sprig of lavender or rosemary for scent and a nice detail. This does take a bit of time, so remember to include the time needed in your spreadsheet (see page 48).

is likely to be) will bring them out to perfection for your reception.

Searing woody plants Cut thick, woody stems of flowers or foliage at a sharp angle with secateurs. Cut up the stem cleanly 5cm (2"), so that you split the stem a little, and then sear it by putting the fresh-cut stem straight into 5cm of boiling water. Cut all the woody stems you need from any one plant into boiling water in this way, then top up the bucket with cold water and leave the stems to condition as you would any other cut material (see page 48). Searing stops plants that have a tendency to wilt from doing so. I find this is particularly needed in the early part of the year, when growth is more sappy.

In addition to woody stems, some other material can be improved by searing, if it has started to flop: wilting roses can be revived, and poppies can be encouraged to stand in water.

If cutting shrubs and woody perennials later on in the season (hydrangeas, for example), when there will be new growth, cut into the new growth (the green stem) and avoid cutting last year's growth (woody, with bark) – then the drinking cells in the stem will be younger and fresher, and better at drinking up water.

Foliage In winter, cut foliage in the mildest part of the day. Foliage cut when frozen solid or covered in snow might defrost to mush if you bring it into warm too quickly. Cut it into buckets of clean water (no need for searing in winter), then let it acclimatize somewhere out of the frost but not in the

Sweet pea tip

If your sweet peas are on stems too short for your floristry purposes, then cut longer sections of the plant, including leaves and curling tendrils: these will give your bigger arrangements interesting texture and shapes as well as the scent of the glorious sweet pea. I often use this technique, especially towards the end of the season, for late-autumn weddings, when sweet-pea stems can be down to 15cm (6") or less.

heat of the house (a log shed, a garage, the back porch), before bringing it into the house for arranging.

In the spring, summer and early autumn, sear foliage stems as described here (see left), and give them a nice long drink before arranging them. I try to cut summer foliage to the length I intend to use it, so that the stems don't need cutting, and therefore searing, again. You'll find that the greener the stem you're cutting, the less searing the foliage needs: new-season growth has sappier stems, which drink water more easily than the previous season's woodier stems.

Count your stems as you cut them, so that you know exactly how many you've got. You will have a plan in which your required stem-count is carefully laid out (see pages 50-1), and you can tick off numbers as you cut. You'll have a lot to do in those last few days before the wedding, so you don't want to waste time cutting more flowers than you need – or, worse, not enough. (See 'How to make a hand-tied posy or bouquet', page 162, for tips on practice posies and bouquets.)

Containers

Cut into tall buckets, scrupulously clean, filled with fresh, clean water. Make sure you have suitable buckets for the job. For example, don't assume that old yard buckets will be good to cut flowers into – they are wider at the neck than at their base, and shorter in height than they are wide, so heavy-headed flowers tend to fall out of them. A bucket that is more or less the same circumference at neck and base, and a good deal taller than it is wide, is more use for conditioning cut flowers in.

Abandon all romantic images you may have of yourself floating about the garden in the sunshine, cutting flowers into a trug. Flowers need to be cut direct into water if they are to perform well for you.

It might be worth investing in a trolley for pulling your buckets about your cut-flower patch and cutting into. Of course, this depends how much you want to spend on what might become something of a growing-cut-flower habit that lasts long after the glories of the wedding day itself.

Here we've used a variety of buckets depending on the stem length of the material we've cut. Sweet peas tend to be shorter-stemmed but abundant, so we use large, deep, rectangular containers and make taped grids across the top, so we can cut the flowers 20 at a time into each section. The container at the front contains 100 sweet peas.

A trolley might be a useful investment: it makes a welcome alternative to a barrow, when you need to transport things on a flat surface to avoid spillage.

A note on skin reactions to plants

There are a few plants that can cause a nasty skin reaction. Whether it be the fine hairs on the flower stems that irritate, or the sap, which might be caustic, do be wary – especially if it's you cutting the flowers for your wedding: you don't want unsightly marks down your arms when you've spent a fortune on that gorgeous sleeveless dress!

Contact dermatitis caused by plants often simply shows up as little red marks on your skin, though these can also blister. So be cautious, and wear long sleeves and gloves when cutting or arranging suspect plants. The reaction is often stronger if handling plant material in sunlight. The following are plants that we have found to cause skin reactions:

- ❧ achillea
- ❧ alchemilla
- ❧ euphorbia
- ❧ hogweed.

Cut bulbs into separate containers. Bulbs weep syrupy sap when they're cut, and this will make the water they're in discolour and fill with bacteria quickly. Let them condition in their own water and then arrange them with other material the next day.

Don't overcrowd your buckets, especially if you're cutting flowers when they're wet or it's raining: the delicate petals of fresh-cut-flowers shoved tightly into a small space will bruise and squash. You've spent a great deal of time and energy growing these flowers, so give them space to condition nicely and they'll be absolutely at their best for your wedding.

Abandon all romantic images you may have of yourself floating about the garden, cutting flowers into a trug. Flowers need to be cut direct into water if they're to perform well.

Conditioning

Put your buckets of flowers somewhere cool, airy and out of direct sunlight for the flowers to condition. A garage, cellar or cool barn would be ideal. Leave your flowers for at least 12 hours or overnight, to have a good long drink (this is when they are being 'conditioned') before you start to arrange them.

Flower food

Should you use flower food? I say not. You are not asking your flowers to last for a month on a sideboard gathering dust, as a sad, much-pulsed-with-sugar-and-bleach imported bunch of gerberas might. You are looking for life, growth, a field of flowers in every posy dancing a celebration of your wedding day. Flowers cut from your garden, following the instructions I've given above, will last happily from Wednesday or Thursday through to Saturday afternoon with nothing but fresh water and clean containers to keep them looking their best. However, if you wish, you *can* make a good home-made flower food in the following way.

Home-made flower food recipe

To 1 litre (1¾ pints) of water add half a teaspoon of sugar, a drop of bleach, and a tiny squeeze of lemon juice (sugar = food; bleach = bacteria killing; lemon juice = pH balancing). Water treated like this will never look crystal clear, and I think that the best way to frame a home-grown bunch of abundant floral beauty is with clean glass and clear water, but you must make your own choice. Perhaps when you make your practice posies (see page 162) you might experiment to see what difference home-made flower food makes to the life of a bunch of your flowers.

Making a plan

This is where I suggest you get really punctilious. You may be rolling your eyes at me, but strict planning is the enemy of last-minute panics, and nobody needs any extra exhausting crises on top of Aunt Betty needing collecting from the airport, Uncle Fred endlessly hovering and asking for jobs to do, and that not-terribly-helpful neighbour dropping in again to chat and drink coffee when you have a wedding to prepare.

The spreadsheet

When I teach growing your own wedding flowers, people look at me in horror when I first bring up the subject of the spreadsheet. They're looking forward to gardening; to admiring the fruits of their labours; to standing back and watching the flowers dance in the breeze – not slaving over Excel

Plan ahead and you'll be able to give your team of helpers strict instructions, so that on the floristry day all goes smoothly and there are no last-minute crises.

on the computer screen. Well, don't panic! There's plenty of time for standing back and admiring too. The spreadsheet can be done well in advance. What it will do for you is inform the schedule of the last few days before the wedding. Although this isn't complicated, it is well worth planning in advance. So draft your spreadsheet, then you can see how many stems you'll need to cut. From this, you can decide how many people you may need to help you cut, store, condition, and then make the flower arrangements. Just to give you an idea, it

takes Sharon, Emily and me 2 hours to cut about 1,000 stems, but we're very fast and efficient. If you're doing a wedding of, say, 650 stems, you'll probably need four or five of you to help.

So your spreadsheet might look like the one on pages 50-51. The numbers it gives are by no means set in stone, but you can see how, if you practise making your posies, etc., you can note how many stems of each variety you need, and translate that into numbers for other stages of the process.

	how many		sweet peas	roses	alchemilla	ox-eye daisies	buttercups	nigella	physocarpus	ammi majus
bride's bouquet	1	30 sweet peas	30							
		10 roses		10						
		5 alchemilla			5					
		5 ox-eye daisies				5				
		5 buttercups					5			
		5 nigella						5		
bridesmaids' posies	3	15 sweet peas	45							
		5 roses		15						
		3 alchemilla			9					
		3 ox-eye daisies				9				
		3 buttercups					9			
		3 nigella						9		
buttonholes	5	1 sweet pea	5							
		1 rose		5						
		1 alchemilla			5					
		1 ox-eye daisy				5				
		1 buttercup					5			
		1 nigella						5		
jam-jar posies	10	5 sweet peas	50							
		3 roses		30						
		3 alchemilla			30					
		1 ox-eye daisy				10				
		3 buttercups					30			
		3 nigella						30		
		3 physocarpus							30	
		3 ammi majus								30
large jugs of flowers	3	10 sweet peas	30							
		10 roses		30						
		5 alchemilla			15					
		5 ox-eye daisies				15				

5 buttercups					15			
5 nigella						15		
5 physocarpus							15	
5 ammi majus								15
10 sweet peas	1 (Pedestal or equivalent)			10				
5 roses			5					
10 alchemilla			10					
5 ox-eye daisies				5				
5 buttercups					5			
15 nigella						15		
10 tall branches of foliage, e.g. physocarpus							10	
15 ammi majus								15
Total number of stems of each flower		170	95	74	49	69	79	55	60
Total number of arrangements	23								
Total number of stems to cut	651								

Checklist	check
Who's cutting Wednesday night	
Who's cutting Thursday night	
Who's helping on Friday	
Who's delivering flowers to venue & ceremony venue & when	
Buckets	
scissors x [number]	
raffia	
ribbon x [how many metres]	
clean, polished jars & containers	
pins	
wire	

Here is an example spreadsheet for an early-summer wedding. A spreadsheet like this can be used to organize all the floristry for your wedding – the timing, the quantities, who's responsible for each activity, etc. You can add more detail: how much ribbon, number of jars, number of tea lights, etc. In this case, as it's not a huge wedding, I haven't split the cutting list into two evenings. But, depending on how much help you have, you might choose to cut the physocarpus, ammi and nigella, for example, on Wednesday evening, and the rest on Thursday evening.

The helpers and the boss

This year I helped two lovely ladies prepare to do the flowers for the wedding of a son. They had ambitious plans, including balls of flowers hanging from the bars criss-crossing the ceiling of the reception venue, garlanding, big flower-foam-based arrangements, and three posies per table for twenty tables at the reception. I suggested they might need more than just the two of them to get all this work done in a day. But they knew each other well and felt that a bigger team might slow them down, and that they'd rather just get on with the job. I still think they could have done with two or three extra helpers.

Ask more people to help than you think you'll need. Arranging wedding flowers is a time-consuming and fiddly business, especially if the people doing it aren't used to arranging flowers very often.

The skill is for one person to take charge, of the planning and the team. A big badge reading 'The Boss' is a cheery joke, but it also reminds everyone of who is directing operations. You, the person in charge, are the one who will have practised making all the arrangements you want to do, and this will inform your planning. It's always very important to practise your floristry in advance when doing your own.

Practise making your posies in advance, and not only will you know how many stems per posy you need, but also you'll be able to show your helpers what you'd like them to do.

Careful planning will ensure that your wedding flowers reflect your dream perfectly.

Wedding helpers love the process of helping with weddings to be exciting. Imposing spreadsheet-style organization on the situation will certainly make the experience less thrilling. However, *you* do not need any more excitement than knowing that the flowers are grown and will be cut, and the floristry will be done in plenty of time before the rehearsal on (say) Friday evening. So impose your will, and your flowers will be cut as you planned and arranged as you'd like, and the day will reflect the dream you have.

The schedule

Work back from the time your wedding ceremony is booked, and think carefully about the time you will have available. If your wedding is to take place on a Saturday afternoon, the chances are that the morning will be taken up with the hairdresser and other last-minute preparations. I recommend that you aim to get as much flower preparation as possible done the day before, so that you're not handling mess-making, water-sloshing, destined-for-the-compost-bin material when there are costly silk and satin dresses about to be spilled upon. Also, whether it's the bride in charge of these lovely home-grown flowers, or her mum, or the groom's mum, it is a fact that every bride needs half an hour on the morning of her wedding for a nervous moment, and in that moment she needs her mum and her girlfriends and sisters to be free to be with her. Nobody needs to be distracted from that crucial time because there are still flowers to be done.

So try to get all flowery business finished before the rehearsal on Friday night – and any flowery work still to be done on the Saturday morning is best delegated to a trusted friend who won't be needed for other important roles.

For the purposes of this book, let's assume your wedding is to take place on Saturday afternoon. If it is to be on another day of the week, simply take the timings I give here, and alter the day names to suit your schedule.

The only jobs you could do on the Saturday morning – and *only* if you'd like to do them then, rather than on Friday – are making the bride's bouquet, the bridesmaids' posies, and perhaps the buttonholes and corsages – but

Buttonholes made the day before will be perfectly happy if left somewhere cool and airy with their stems in water overnight before the wedding.

I would really heartily recommend that you try to have these made by Friday night. A wander round the garden deadheading roses into a basket on the Saturday morning will also give you fresh petal confetti. However, all of these jobs can be done on the Friday, and I would say that, if you can, you'd do better to get all the floristry done on the Friday. I will admit I hate rushing, and will do anything to avoid a last-minute fluster of any kind. If you like the adrenaline rush of doing things at the last minute, then by all means plan to make your bouquet on the Saturday morning!

If you're to do all the floristry on the Friday, you'll need to have all your flowers cut by Thursday evening, so that they can spend the night having a nice drink before being arranged.

Cutting and conditioning countdown

Wednesday evening
- Cut foliage and filler. Leave to condition in clean buckets of fresh water.

Thursday evening
- Cut all flower stems.
- Put to one side, clearly labelled, the flowers you'll use for the bride, bridesmaids and buttonholes.
- Leave all flowers and foliage to condition in tall, clean buckets of fresh water until you're ready to arrange them on Friday.

Friday
- Start arranging your flowers in the morning. Do the ceremony flowers first, then the reception flowers, then the buttonholes and the bride's and bridesmaids' bouquets. Make the bride's bouquet last, because you'll become very practised through the day. Try to get all the arrangements finished on Friday.
- If you can install the flowers in the venue on Friday, do so, but only if the venue is cool. A hot tent overnight won't do flowers any good. If your ceremony or reception will take place in a marquee, then I suggest you keep the flowers somewhere cool the night before and only install them on the Saturday morning.
- Large arrangements can be spritzed with water to keep them looking fresh.

Saturday
- If the weather's hot, then the flowers might do well to have fresh water on the morning of the wedding: not only will this keep them fresher, but in hot weather flower water can go yellow, which isn't as attractive in glass as perfectly clear, clean water.

Wednesday and Thursday

At Common Farm, we cut flowers all day long, all year round. It takes three of us about 2 hours to cut 1,000 stems. You will be nothing like so speedy with your scissors, so I suggest the following schedule.

Cut the foliage for your wedding flowers on Wednesday evening, and the flowers on Thursday. Two hundred stems of foliage cut on Wednesday can sit happily in buckets until Friday. Four hundred stems of flowers is a perfectly manageable number for you and perhaps two or three friends to cut together on Thursday evening. Give each of your helpers a list of what you need them to cut, and strict instructions as to how you want them to cut – stem length, how open your flowers should be, and so on – and you can all set off to cut the flowers, leaving somebody else to cook you supper and provide a cool glass of wine when you've finished.

Practice makes perfect. If you've practised cutting and tying and arranging some samples of your flowers (see 'How to make a hand-tied posy or bouquet', page 162), you'll know how much time you need to schedule in advance of doing the whole event, and you can plan your floristry accordingly. I've said Wednesday and Thursday evening, but if you're planning a smaller wedding you may be able to cut it all on Thursday

Large arrangements can be spritzed with water to keep them looking ding-dong fresh - as if they've just been cut in a dew-drenched dawn.

evening. For a much bigger wedding, you'll need more pairs of hands to help, because you don't really want to be cutting your fresh garden flowers on Tuesday and expecting them to be perfect for the wedding on Saturday.

Friday

So now all your flowers are cut. Your cool, airy, out-of-direct-sunlight place is filled

You do not need any more excitement than knowing that the flowers are grown and will be cut, and that the floristry will be done in plenty of time before the rehearsal.

with buckets of smiley flowery faces. If you're going to make the bride's bouquet and the bridesmaids' posies and button-holes, put the ingredients for those to one side and make sure they are clearly labelled, so an overenthusiastic helper can't possibly use them to make posies for the portaloos.

Where to do the floristry?

I would advise that you do the floristry all in one place: somewhere cool and airy and out of direct sunlight. Don't expect flowers to do well if you plan to arrange them in full sun outside in the heat of the day.

You'll need a large clean surface for arranging on, and space to put the flowers when they've been done – another table, or a sideboard. You'll also need something in which to transport the flowers to the venue: low-sided trays, such as old mushroom trays or baker's trays, are ideal. Higher-sided boxes or crates might be needed to transport taller arrangements.

Don't plan to arrange your flowers at the venue: you'll be double handling buckets and vases, you'll make a mess you'll have to clear up, and you may not be allowed to get into the venue until the day of the wedding – and you don't want to be doing flowers so last-minute. Decide well in advance where the floristry will be done, and arrange the space to fit your needs. You may find that your neighbour's house is better than yours, or that the garage, or a barn space if you have access to one, is ideal.

Timing

Start early. You will need more time than you think. Try to get the ceremony venue flowers done first, and if they're to be used in a cool, stone church, you could send somebody off to deliver them and get them out of the way.

Do the table-centre posies and other reception arrangements next.

If you have a big enough team of helpers, then you can leave them to get on with all the above, so that you can do the bride's

Collect useful-sized trays in which to transport your flowers when they're ready.

Once the flowers are done, put them somewhere cool and airy until it's time to carry them down the aisle.

Roses cut on the Thursday for a Saturday wedding will be half as open as this when cut. This photograph was taken on the Friday, after the bouquet was made. The rose would be fully open and perfect for the wedding ceremony.

bouquet, bridesmaids' posies and button-holes. Have vases, jugs or jars ready for the bouquets and buttonholes to be put in once they're finished. *Plan* to be finished by mid afternoon, and then you *will* be finished by late afternoon.

Once the flowers are finished, take time to stand back and admire them. You'll have done a wonderful job and saved yourself a merry fortune. Well done!

Top cutting and conditioning tips

- Use clean scissors; clean buckets; fresh water. Bacteria are enemies of the cut flower.

- Cut bulbs into their own containers, and keep separate from the other material until the next day.

- In winter, cut foliage in the most clement part of the day.

- In warm weather, cut in the morning or evening. Never cut flowers or foliage when you can feel the heat of the sun on the back of your neck.

- Cut straight into water, so that the cellulose cells which sponge water up to the flower head never have time to dry up and stop working.

- To keep the flower water clean, in hot weather you might want to add a drop of bleach to it to stop bacteria growing and spoiling the perfection of the flowers. We don't recommend any kind of flower food, sugar, or dropping pennies in the water – though if that's what your grandmother suggests, go with her – I wouldn't want to try teaching anybody to suck eggs.

- Leave flowers to have a nice long drink (condition) once they're cut. Overnight is perfect. Then they'll be ready to be used in your floristry the next day.

PART TWO
PLANNING FOR YOUR WEDDING

A SPRING WEDDING

With the natural world beginning to pounce into life, blossom opening and leaves unfurling, spring brings a world full of promise, hope and possibility: a great time to be married. And you can really take advantage of the season and enjoy a delicacy in your wedding flowers that may not be so easy to achieve later in the summer. From bluebells to tulips, cow parsley to lilac, apple blossom to aquilegia, the colours can be muted and delicate, the flowers wild, and you can be daring in the floral mixtures you use.

Whatever the time of year you are to be married, the first thing to do when planning your flower scheme is to look at what was in flower on that date the previous year (and the year before, and the year before that. . .). If your wedding is more than a year away, this is easier to do in the first instance, but it's still worth taking the time to think back, and to talk to other experienced local gardeners, to work out which plants can be relied on.

What's in the garden already?

Be sure to plan your wedding flowers around what you can forage from estab-lished gardens and other areas that are available to you, as well as on what you can grow. There will certainly be some good material to be found locally without your having to grow it all.

Fruit blossom

Fruit blossom goes over very quickly, so I wouldn't advise basing your wedding flowers on the apple trees in the gardens you may have available to you. However, do be oppor-tunistic, because fruit blossom is stunning, whether arranged as cushions in a vintage soup bowl as a table centre, or in tall sprays to frame the reception entrance. You can force tree blossom by taking prunings from mid winter and bringing them into the

A cheerful mix of narcissi and tulips in a vintage pedestal vase is a happy combination for a simple table centre.

We have cut buttercups with a scythe at times, but even a handful brings a burst of sunshine into a spring posy.

This spring bride's bouquet has apple blossom, cow parsley, cowslips and wild bluebells in it – all already growing in the garden before the tulips were planted for the wedding.

The mix of what you might find in a spring garden might surprise you if you think about it. From apple blossom to forget-me-nots; to wild red campion, to bluebells, to cow parsley – here we even have early rose foliage, red edged and deliciously glossy, to use as greenery in a bride's bouquet.

house. Put the stems in containers with a little water (which you must keep refreshed from time to time) and watch the blossom fatten up and begin to unfold. It's difficult to control when the blossom will come out, but even if it isn't out yet, the knobbly drama of lichened old apple-tree prunings makes a lovely frame to use as a base for your spring wedding floristry.

Tree and shrub foliage

Depending on the date of your wedding, you'll have wonderful foliage of some sort exploding into leaf all over the place. I particularly love the acid-green fireworks of flowering oak, which are stunning mixed into an arrangement with cow parsley and tulips. Balsam poplar has a gorgeous scent that is reminiscent of honey, because bees use the stickiness of the buds to make propolis, with which they glue their hives together – but don't use too much, because the smell can be overwhelming. Grey poplar has silvery leaves on silvery stems, while hornbeam and beech leaves will unfurl in the vase to make lovely delicate shapes in your floristry.

Apple blossom will happily be forced into flower when brought into a warm room.

Lilac will last much better in a cut-flower arrangement if the stems are seared when it is cut.

Keep an eye on all your shrubs and hedge-rows: in spring they're bursting with good-ies that make good material for cutting. They may look dormant one week but be breaking into life the next. A few stems from any tree which looks as though it'll be in leaf very soon – with fat, swelling buds on the stems – can be encouraged to leaf early by being brought inside into the warm.

Lilac can be lovely if it is in flower for your wedding, but be sure to sear it when you cut it (see Chapter 3, page 45), to stop it wilting. I find that spring, when many plants have fresh, sappy growth, is a time when I need to sear more than at any other time of year. With lilac, you should strip all the foliage bar the 'bow tie' of leaves just below the flowering head. Then snip the stem at a sharp angle and cut cleanly up it for a couple of inches before plunging the cut end into boiling water for 30 seconds or so.

Some people are very superstitious about lilac and won't have it in the house. Person-ally, I like to absolve any flower from unfor-tunate superstitious associations – which are hardly fair on the flower. What did lilac do to deserve such a bad reputation? But do check with Granny too, in case she has strong feelings on the matter and is likely to react alarmingly when she sees armfuls of lilac used in your wedding flowers.

Also flowering in late spring or early summer, the snowball bush (cousin of the wild guelder rose) gives us its fabulous spheres of greenish-white blooms. If the viburnum beetle doesn't get its leaves, then the foliage is as useful – very fresh and green – as the flowers. It's perhaps better for larger arrangements than for posies (just because it's so useful as tall structure, and you might want to use the foliage as well as the balls of flowers), but don't overlook it.

This very simple bride's posy has just-unfurling *Spiraea japonica* 'Goldflame' in it. (The bride didn't really want to carry anything at all but I persuaded her that a tiny mix like this would give her something to do with her hands.) Without good conditioning that lovely foliage would wilt in a heartbeat.

Look out too for flowering physocarpus (both the dark red and acid-green varieties), and the wild viburnum, the wayfaring tree, which has a very pretty flat umbellifer flower. All of the above will benefit from searing before use in floristry.

Some people hate its stink, but we also use choisya, which has wonderful glossy, ever-green foliage. We find that the smell disappears quickly after cutting and that it's only the bruising of the stem in the cutting that makes for a short-lived unpleasantness.

Perennials

Aquilegia (columbine, or granny's bonnets) flowers for almost 2 months from mid to late spring. Bistort, irises, early alliums . . . the garden is full of offerings at this time of year. Here at Common Farm, we use a great

Jam-jar posies ready for transporting to the wedding venue. These include a lot of wildflowers and freshly unfurling foliage, for a bride who wanted a very wild look to her flowers.

deal of the lovely dramatic, dark foliage of 'Firecracker' loosestrife in spring, to frame our floristry.

Do practise your arrangements in advance (see Part 3), to see if any of the ingredients you're planning to use are likely to wilt. This is especially important in spring, as at this time of year the sappy growth can make plant stems very prone to flopping. Try searing wilty herbaceous cuttings, as you would for woody material (see Chapter 3, page 45), to see if they'll stand up for you – it's well worth making sure beforehand, rather than assuming that all will be well on your wedding day. That said, after an overnight drink in a bucket, floppy spring growth will often revive.

Wildflowers

Cowslips, cow parsley, red campion, forget-me-nots, buttercups, tellima, cuckoo flower (lady's smock), wild snake's head fritillaries . . . the meadows and hedgerows are full of flowers to cut in spring. It is perhaps the richest time of year for wildflowers. When brides call me and say "I'm getting married in late summer, and I want wildflowers everywhere," my heart sinks slightly, as I know it'll be a tougher forage for flowers that haven't turned into seedheads. In spring, on the other hand, I know there will be an abundance.

Spring-flowering wildflowers are often perennial – all of the list above are, save forget-me-nots (biennial) and fritillaries (bulbs). They can also be very fussy about where they grow. You *could* buy them all as plants

We have found cowslips to be easy to grow from seed.

and put them in the ground the autumn before your wedding – tellima certainly makes a lovely border plant in the long term. Of the spring wildflowers, I'd say cowslips are the easiest to grow from seed – if you have enough notice, and can sow the seed the summer before you need them to flower. We grow cowslips to cut, and their scent in spring bouquets is one of my favourites during the whole cut-flower year. (See Resources section for a good supplier of UK native wildflower seed.)

However, it is often the case that wildflowers prefer that unexpected corner under a hedge; the edge of a meadow; the wild grass in the

This tiny posy is made up of cowslips and cuckoo flower. The cowslips have a gorgeous, slightly bergamot scent, but the cuckoo flower does smell a bit cabbagey. I don't mind this edge to the scent, but you may not love it. This posy is just inches high and wide – exquisite, but it won't make a great focal point to your wedding scheme.

orchard. In order to avoid disappointment, it might be best to identify in advance good swathes of the wildflowers you'd like to cut for your wedding, and if they are on land which doesn't belong to you, then seek permission to cut them. Establishing enough cow parsley from scratch to cut for a wedding scheme could be very stressful; helping yourself from the half-mile of it edging the neighbouring farm may be the easier option.

Weddings are often stressful occasions, with brides and grooms conscious that everyone's looking at them – which is the point, but can still make one self-conscious when the actual moment of declaration looms. A single buttercup can give the nervous couple something gorgeous to look at; a distraction from the well-wishing crowd. I've had brides tell me that on the journey to the ceremony they just focused on the buttercup I put in their bouquet, and all the pressure disappeared and they

THE BELTANE FLOWER

In the wild hedge you'll also find hawthorn, or the May flower. You know that saying, 'Ne'er cast a clout till May be out'? Well, that's referring to hawthorn, which, in the UK at least, can flower earlier than May, and sometimes later. (The saying means 'Don't shed your winter clothes till the hawthorn is flowering.') This lovely blossom and its leaves, which people eat as 'hedge salad' when they're just unfurling, is also known as the Beltane flower, and in pagan times they would have made the original flower crowns with it and celebrated marriages using May flowers for all the decorations.

But do cut wildflowers last?

Some people say that wildflowers don't last once cut. Allow me to differ. Cut wildflowers directly into water, when the day is still cool, and even buttercups should last a week. It's true that wild-flowers have more delicate stems than some of their cultivar cousins – but that means, simply, that one must take a little more care cutting them. Wildflowers in any season won't take kindly to being kept out of water, and so won't do well for long in flower-foam-based arrangements, but for a day or so they'll be fine – although they are more difficult to use in flower foam because their stems tend to be too delicate for any pushing.

These wildflower buttonholes are in tiny phials of water to keep them fresh until the very last minute.

remembered that the day was just about them, and their betrothed, and about their plighting their troth. Everything else – the table plan, the chair bows, the bridesmaids' dresses, Great Aunt Winifred's querulous request to sit as far away from her sister as possible – just faded into insignificance.

Of course, I do not advocate any kind of larceny: it is illegal to cut wildflowers in the UK from road verges, as this land belongs to the local council, and you shouldn't steal from fields, even if the flowers are wild. But ask, and the farmer's likely to say yes to you: who wouldn't allow a bride a handful of buttercups for her bouquet?

What to grow

For a spring wedding, you'll need to get your planting done in the autumn of the previous year. There are so many options to choose from, but (whatever the season) I'd suggest you aim to have between five and seven types of flower in your arrangements and posies, along with any other goodies you have been able to find that are in flower at the time of your ceremony.

Work out how many stems you're going to need before you plant (see Chapter 1, page 21) – you don't need to be too exact, but it's useful to know whether it's 300, 600, 1,000 . . .

Wildflowers are difficult to use in flower-foam floristry because their stems tend to be too delicate for any pushing.

This bride's bouquet is made up of lots of interesting tulips, which are not the sort you'd easily find in inexpensive bunches at your local florist or supermarket. The cream double, especially, which is called 'Verona', has the most delicious lemony vanilla scent.

You might allow the colours of the bulb flowers to influence the colours of your wedding. I'm a great fan of the cowslip / white narcissus / ballet-shoe-pink mix – but you may prefer rich purples or bright tulip pinks.

Bulbs

Bulbs are the obvious flower to plant for spring weddings. There are myriad different shapes and colours to tempt you: from scented narcissi to subtle ornithogalum; from huge-headed Darwin Hybrid tulips to delicate bluebells, from snake's head fritillaries to bold, tall irises. Take your time looking through the bulb catalogues and think about how you can best use your space and budget. Bulbs can be expensive, and part of the point of growing your own wedding flowers is that you'll save a good deal of money. I have to admit that it's difficult not to go mad with a bulb catalogue, as there's so much to entice you.

Your bulbs will be much better quality (and considerably better value) if ordered directly from wholesalers, whether online or through mail-order catalogues. Wholesalers these days will sell to anyone who wants to buy, not just the trade – the price just gets better the more you order. Bulbs from wholesalers will have been kept in optimum conditions and be just right for planting. Not only that, but a good supplier (see Resources section

Choose bulbs for scent, for shape and size, and for the fact that you can't buy those flowers elsewhere for less than it will cost you to grow them. Grow more unusual varieties, which will be expensive to buy cut.

Anemones in a wildflower wedding mix, with forget-me-nots and white deadnettle as well as honesty, cow parsley and cowslips.

for recommendations) will give you excellent advice on varieties to grow and what will be in flower when. Some bulb catalogues are arranged so that you can see all the kinds of bulbs that will flower together throughout spring – very helpful if you're not sure about what combinations will work well.

Do tell the supplier *when* you'd like your bulbs to be delivered, otherwise they may come too early for you to be ready to plant.

Choose bulbs for scent, for shape and size (biggest isn't always best . . .), and for the fact that you can't buy those flowers elsewhere

for less than it will cost you to grow them. By this I mean that planting a sack of cheap daffs or narcissi may not be cheaper than buying them as cut-flower stems, even still relatively locally grown. Grow more unusual varieties, which will be expensive to buy cut.

Anemones

Don't forget these delicate little round-petalled, daisy-shaped flowers. They come in all sorts of colours, from sapphire blues and ruby reds to whites and to creams with delicate pinkish edges. Their button-like centres remind me of Victorian frogging for a gentleman's smoking jacket. They can be short-stemmed, but they work very well bunched in posies and in jam jars. If you have some space in a polytunnel or green-house, then growing them under cover will have them flowering earlier, though don't forget to feed and water them. Give them seaweed solution once they begin to bud up, to achieve better stem length and lots of repeat-flowering.

Bluebells

Spanish bluebells have a stronger head, with more flowers, than the UK native bluebell, but they hybridize with our native bluebell and set seed in the wild, so I prefer to grow the delicate, native stock. You're unlikely to be able to grow masses of bluebells in time for your wedding, because they're often sold 'in the green' – freshly dug up in clumps after flowering, in late spring. But if you have a friend with a patch of bluebells in their garden, or you have permission to cut some from a nearby wood, then a handful of these beauties in a bride's bouquet is just stunning.

This is a 'pew end' posy attached to a chair. If you do attach jam-jar posies in this way, use a little Blu-tack to stop it swinging and spilling water on your guests. This posy can later be used as a table centrepiece.

Grape hyacinths work well in buttonholes, posies and elsewhere, but they are short-stemmed, so don't expect them to be any use in tall arrangements.

Grape hyacinths

Your mother may shoot you if you say you'd like to plant a lot of this often-invasive bulb variety, but for value for money and that lovely, perfect true blue, grape hyacinths (muscari) make a very good wedding flower. Giving sharp little uprights for buttonholes, dots of blue for bouquets – if you don't have bluebells, grape hyacinths make a good alternative. Look for taller varieties, to get a bit more stem length for your posies.

Irises

For great height and structure, do plant some irises. They'll last a week in water if you cut them when the colour is just showing at the tip of the top flower. However, for wedding flowers, wait until they're more open than that. You need wedding flowers to last 2 or 3 days from cutting, and be fully open for the event itself, not just stand in a vase for a week. The bearded iris flowers later than the traditional-for-cutting Dutch iris – too late for a spring wedding. But Dutch irises planted in autumn will flower beautifully for you the following spring. The pure white with a lemon tongue is gorgeously spring-like.

Ornithogalum

I'm a great fan of this grey-and-white scilla-like flower, known often as star of Bethlehem. For a pale, silvery-grey, vintage look, this

Grey-and-white ornithogalum is stunning in this buttonhole with one tulip, an anemone, lime foliage and a spray of spiraea leaf.

makes an unusual flower, which your guests might not have seen before. As with fritillaries and grape hyacinths, pull rather than cut the stems in order to get more stem length for use in your posies.

Ranunculus

For brides who would like a rose shape in springtime, the ranunculus is the perfect alternative to a real rose. I often use ranunculus in spring floristry, and am surprised at how frequently I'm asked which rose they are. Plant them under cover if you can, for an early crop, but they'll flower happily outside in a protected patch, perhaps in the shelter of a warm wall. Choose interesting colours: there are lovely white varieties with pink and purple picotee edges, as well as bright yellows and oranges and tall, floaty whites. Also known as Persian buttercups, they like free-draining soil, but will get

"WHO GIVES THIS WOMAN TO BE WED?"

This question was asked of fathers, or the male head of a family, in the days when marriages were arranged between families, and brides didn't necessarily have a choice. The line is often changed now, as the person who 'gives away' the bride can be a mum, a brother, a sister, a grandparent – whoever the bride chooses to accompany her down the aisle.

Ranunculus in a spring mix does the job that a rose or peony might do later in the season.

mildew if they dry out too much, so do remember to water as well as feed them if they're under cover.

Snake's head fritillaries

Associated with ancient meadows, the wild snake's head fritillary is cheap to buy as a bulb (or 100 bulbs), and makes a surprisingly good cut flower. Be aware, though, that when you put 100 bulbs into the ground, you may only get 20 or 30 flowering stems: mice will have your fritillary bulbs, and birds will have the flowers if they can. We find that fritillaries do much better in the sward of the orchard than in a raised bed,

A snake's head fritillary used in a mix of spring flowers gives the whole mix an unusual look.

A bride's posy of tulips, narcissi, grape hyacinths and early-season foliage. The scent is as gorgeous as the look.

though if you only want perhaps five or six for the bride's bouquet, then by all means just put them in a mouse-and-bird-proofable pot and grow them that way.

Pull the stems rather than cut them, and you'll get longer stems to use in posies. The stems of these delicate flowers are very fragile, so support them in posies with other foliage and flowers around them, to stop the fritillaries from collapsing. We find they grow much more happily in a meadow situation (as they would in the wild) than in beds where, without much competition, they can be too short-stemmed even for little posies.

Tulips

For size of flower, strong structure, variety of colour and (perhaps surprisingly) height, tulips are a great idea to grow for wedding flowers. Whether you choose a scheme of, say, pure white or rich purples and oranges, there will be a tulip to give you the colour you want to build your wedding look around. If you'd like accessories to match your flowers, then your tulip colour is a great basis from which to choose table runners, chair bows or ribbons. Just a few tulips in a wildflower posy give it good structure, and something stronger for the delicate wildflowers to frame. Equally, three tall

Container bulbs

If you're planting bulbs as part of your scheme, plant some in containers too. These make lovely displays, which you can simply put in place all in one piece without cutting them to dress your wedding. Attractively potted-up tulips look stunning either side of the church door, while wooden crates of flowering anemones will give a farmers'-market look to your scheme.

In addition, smaller containers can be used as table centrepieces. Plant up teacups with miniature narcissi and grape hyacinths, dot them down the table centres, with jars of pussy willow to give the scheme height, and your wedding will be a gorgeous mix of miniature gardens.

Pots of planted-up flowering bulbs can be put in and out of warmth to get them flowering at the right time. Or, if all else fails, they can be bought at the garden centre at the last minute!

Pure white narcissus 'Thalia', with her gorgeous scent, flowering in the first year after being planted the previous autumn.

tulips in a vintage bottle look gorgeous as a really simple table decoration. The huge-headed Darwin Hybrids open out beautifully when brought into the warm, and will be as dramatic as peonies or roses in a spring scheme.

As I said in Chapter 1, you could simply plant 500 tulips and have your whole wedding done that way. The challenge is to choose tulips that will definitely be in flower for your wedding date. Take good advice: look at the bulb catalogues, and talk to the bulb suppliers – they are generally very helpful. Some tulips start flowering quite early, while others go on until the first roses are out – so you need to choose varieties that suit your date.

Plant some bulbs in containers too. These make lovely displays, which you can simply put in place all in one piece without cutting them to dress your wedding. And smaller containers can be used as table centrepieces.

Planting bulbs for cutting

Planting bulbs for cutting is a different business from planting bulbs for naturalizing in beds or even in long grass. If you order in a good lot of bulbs to grow for a wedding, then you could plant them in beds almost shoulder to shoulder and not necessarily as deeply as you might for naturalizing. They won't take up too much space and will be close to one another for convenient cutting, and then after they've flowered you might move them to somewhere else to naturalize (settle in and flower year after year) or give them away to people who've been helpful.

Remember that if you plan for the bulbs to flower again next year, you have to be careful not to cut the foliage when you cut the flowers. The plants will need to absorb goodness from the foliage for the bulbs to use as food for the following year's flowering. If, however, you really are just growing for your wedding, then you needn't worry and can use the foliage in your arrangements. Flower farmers tend to treat tulips, in particular, as annuals, as the bulbs are relatively cheap. They'll pull the whole bulb out of the ground when cutting, and discard the bulb straight on to the compost heap when the flowering stem is conditioning in a bucket. This may seem harsh, but it's certainly a speedy way to handle cutting flowers for your wedding.

Biennials

I talk about biennials in detail in the next chapter, because they'll be more reliably flowering in early summer. I'm writing this as we come into mid spring, and, while I am cutting a few wallflowers, and the Icelandic poppies are budding up, the rest of my biennials are still weeks and weeks away from flowering. So, if you're in a warm spot and your wedding is in late spring, biennials are a possibility, and by all means look at the biennials section in Chapter 5 to help you decide whether to include them in your scheme – but for most spring weddings I wouldn't count on them.

Hardy annuals

I mention hardy annuals here only to say that for a spring wedding I wouldn't invest time in trying to grow them to be in flower for your big day. If you're an experienced grower and have some space under cover, then you might try to have sweet peas and cornflowers ready for a wedding in spring, but I think there's plenty of other material to work with, and, if I were you, I'd focus on the kinds of plants I've described in the preceding pages. Your time is limited, and the amount of stress you put on yourself should be carefully controlled. After all, a wedding is a day to be looked forward to for its joy and laughter, not with dread because your sweet peas don't look as though they'll be in flower yet.

If you really want to have hardy annuals in flower for a spring wedding, do look at the next chapter for information on autumn sowing of hardy annuals.

Top tips for spring wedding flowers

- As in any season, aim for about five to seven types of flower, plus other goodies you can find. For a spring wedding, a basic ingredients list of, say, tulips, narcissi, cowslips, ornithogalum and grape hyacinths can be dotted about with occasional precious heads of fritillaries, bluebells, the first aquilegias, fruit-tree blossom, oak leaves . . .

- When ordering your bulbs from the wholesaler, remember to say when you'd like them to be delivered, so you're ready for them.

- Do plant some bulbs in attractive pots. These can be brought indoors to force the flowers to open earlier, if necessary. Put them at the entrance to the ceremony venue, or to frame the ceremony itself, and use smaller containers as table centrepieces.

- Spring cut flowers may be a little floppy (wilty) with sappy new growth. Be prepared to sear floppy stems, and practise your cutting technique, so that you can be confident that after a night of good conditioning, your flower stems will be upright again and ready for arranging.

- Spring bulbs can be short-stemmed. Pull them gently from the ground, and you'll get several inches more stem length than if you cut them.

Wildflower buttonholes are gorgeous for a spring wedding.

Flowers arranged using a wide range of bulbs planted the previous autumn and flowering just on time.

A SPRING WEDDING AT A GRAND OLD HOUSE ON THE SOMERSET LEVELS

This bride and groom wanted really wild-looking posies for their mid-spring wedding, and, despite the grandeur of the venue (one of the oldest continuously inhabited houses in the whole of the UK, with parts of it dating back to the fourteenth century), I think the posies worked well. After all, old houses become part of the landscape, and these wild, herby, tussy-mussy-style posies look wonderful in the light of these old rooms. The ceremony took place in a beautiful ballroom, which was then transformed for the wedding breakfast.

A posy of spring wildflowers like this one will need careful conditioning before being used for floristry. A lot of sappy new growth means they can be floppy when cut. But when it works . . . very pretty.

A buttonhole of white pear blossom and herb foliage is beautiful, but it won't last in the warmth all day. You could make a spare for the groom if you plan to have more photographs when his first buttonhole may be struggling.

The bride was clever with her budget and chose to turn the bridesmaids' and her own bouquet into table centrepieces after the ceremony. This would be an efficient way to keep down the number of stems you need to cut and arrange yourself if you're growing your own.

The flowers for this wedding were based on a wild, green background, and were all cut from what was available – just the best in the garden on the day. This meant that the colours had a real garden feel, and the arrangements didn't look too 'designed'. Very fresh.

The groom's buttonhole had a single white bluebell, pear blossom, and early-season foliage. It was beautiful against his French blue suit.

The posies were recycled into table centrepieces using blue glass Mason jars, of which the bride had found a boxful at a flea market some months before.

This wedding, at Maunsel House near Taunton, was photographed by Bath-based photographer Howell Jones Photography (www.howelljonesphotography.co.uk).

CHAPTER FIVE

AN EARLY SUMMER WEDDING

Roses, peonies, daisies, irises, sweet peas, cornflowers, alchemilla . . . This is the time to be married if you dream of being framed by a Fragonard of roses. The cornucopia of delight in the early-summer garden is romantic, full of colour and heady with scent. I look at a big, early-summer wedding scheme when I've cut it, and it seems almost absurd in its lushness.

Early summer – time for what we call the full Fragonard of roses wedding.

When you're planning, think carefully. Manage your expectations, and you will be thrilled by the results.

With autumn sowing of hardy annuals to set you up with a good crop, and some judicious re-sowing early in the year to bulk up your stock in case you need it, you can do a whole wedding in early summer with just annuals. Biennials will be flowering if you planned far enough in advance to get them in the previous year. But even without biennials, a space the size of an allotment bed, cleared and sown with annuals early in the previous autumn, can supply flowers for a whole wedding. And don't forget the perennials: if you have roses you can use, if there are peonies in Grandma's garden, then it would be a shame to waste them.

So when you're planning, remember those 600 stems I spoke of in Chapter 1, and think carefully. Imagine how many roses you really can get from your garden, and how many peonies from Grandma's. Remember that peonies don't flower for long (although their foliage is always useful), and that you can't guarantee when roses will begin to

A small wedding scheme cut and conditioning on a bench in the shade.

A bouquet made with roses, philadelphus, flowering annuals and one late buttercup. I'm a great fan of not being too matchy-matchy with flowers, and this is a great mix of brights for a classic cottage-garden look.

A good-sized patch of ammi majus to cut will give you lots of lacy froth with which to frame your flowers.

bloom. Don't look at two rose bushes and imagine you'll have a hundred roses. You might have five or ten good ones for the day. So plan accordingly. Keep the roses for your bride's bouquet, and maybe one each for the bridesmaids. Manage your expectations, and you will be thrilled by the results.

Thankfully, in early summer, the masses of annuals you'll have sown for the occasion will fill any space left by over-early peonies, or not-quite-abundant-enough roses. A good patch of ammi majus, sown direct or in trays the previous autumn, or even direct-sown in early spring, will be flowering now and give you clouds of white lace with which to frame your wedding. Cornflowers sown in early autumn will be in full flower, while those sown in early spring will be just beginning to be at their best.

What's in the garden already?

If you're able to start planning a full year before your wedding date, look at the established gardens available to you and make a list of what you might use from them. Is there a path edged with alchemilla, thyme

Foliage

At this time of year, shrubby foliage in the garden can still be a bit hit-and-miss to condition. Do practise conditioning shrubby greenery before using it (see Chapter 3, page 45), to make sure you're confident that you can keep it standing well for the day or three you'll need it for your wedding flowers. I do think greenery is necessary in floristry: it not only helps separate the flowers in the bouquet so that you can see them, but also gives the arrangement a depth of field. To my mind, floristry is really just about making miniature gardens – and only in rather dread schemes of municipal planting are you likely to find flowerbeds with no greenery. The best country-house herbaceous borders are framed with greenery, and so are the best bouquets.

In early summer there's beginning to be a mass of greenery in the garden – not only tree and shrub foliage, but also from herbaceous perennials. Who do you know with an established patch of alchemilla? This is perhaps my favourite greenery of all. If you don't have ready access to a good supply of foliage or don't trust your shrubby greenery not to wilt, for an early-summer wedding you could grow bupleurum and euphorbia oblongata. Both hardy, both will flower from an autumn sowing. If they are to be your only greenery, then you might grow quite a lot of them: perhaps twice as much as you would for each of the flowers you're going to use.

And for more, different kinds of foliage, be creative with what's available: ammi visnaga has wonderful foliage, which looks great in cut flowers; nigella has gorgeous, sharply

---

FLOWER MEANINGS

There are so many meanings associated with flowers, and often the sources are contradictory. I always choose the nicest meaning – and here are a few:

- 🌸 dahlias: for a proud moment
- 🌸 daisies: for loyal love
- 🌸 ears of corn: for fecundity
- 🌸 honeysuckle: for constant devotion
- 🌸 ivy: for fidelity
- 🌸 myrtle: ancient symbol of marriage
- 🌸 oak: for strength
- 🌸 rosemary: for remembrance
- 🌸 roses:
  - orange/apricot for passion
  - pink for love and gratitude
  - red for love and romance
  - white for marriage
  - yellow for joy and good health
- 🌸 sunflowers: for loyalty and longevity
- 🌸 sweet peas: for having a lovely time.

---

or catmint? Are there tall spires of delphiniums at the back of the border? Are there roses that you could cut for your bride's and bridesmaids' bouquets? Lamb's ears for framing posies and giving a velvety background to the buttonholes? And what colour are the flowers you can use? There: now you have the backbone, the main palette of your colour scheme, and you can sow annuals to work with what you already have.

Tiny acid-green flowers of bupleurum conditioning with sweet pea 'Painted Lady'. The bupleurum gives the pinks and whites of this scheme a background to shine against.

cut foliage, which works especially well in buttonholes, as it's not wilty. All of the late-season perennials will be shooting strongly, even if they're not yet in flower – cut these strong shoots for your floristry, and you'll be giving your garden a handy Chelsea chop (a little late, but the plants won't mind) at the same time.

Remember to look at the silver-coloured foliage in your garden as well. Perhaps you could cut that artemisia your Aunty Mary has edging her hot, dry bed. Lamb's ears has not only lovely silver foliage but also interesting spikes of velvety silver flowers. And soft, silvery cineraria, with its lovely cut-out shapes, is a favourite with brides.

Hosta leaves, in all their interesting varieties of colour, collar bouquets and posies beautifully (so long as the slugs haven't got at them). And don't forget the herbs: mint is great as foliage, thyme is short-stemmed but lovely in posies and will very likely be in flower at this time of year, and rosemary gives you gorgeous, sharply scented spikes of shape and structure for your bouquets.

Wildflowers

There will be red campion in the hedgerows, buttercups in the fields, ox-eye daisies and lovely coppery wild sorrel seedheads to cut for wild ingredients in wedding flowers. The red valerian will be flowering, and wild foxgloves too. Meadow cranesbill is beautiful to look at, but almost impossible to condition successfully, so I'd leave that where it is. Equally, unless you have a personal, private swathe of orchids, perhaps leave these rare beauties – which are re-establishing themselves around our once over-poisoned land, but slowly. Ox-eye daisies are delightful in flower arrangements; however, do be wary of using too many of them, as they make the water they sit in stink as though a cat has peed in the house.

Wildflowers do cut and stand happily in water, although they are more delicate than their cultivar cousins. They tend to have fragile stems that are easy to bruise or snap, so they're difficult to use in flower-foam floristry. It's best to use them in water rather than try to get the stems into flower foam (see Chapter 4, page 69).

Wildflower growing

The wildflowers I've mentioned above are all perennial. We grow them by sowing the seed in trays in early summer the year before we expect them to flower, and then planting out the seedlings in the autumn. We grow red campion and ox-eye daisies in flowerbeds. Be warned, though, that if you do this they will invade the space they're given. We cut both by the armful through the season, but if you want only a few stems to give your posies a wild feel, you may be better off keeping an eye out for a wild patch from which you can cut opportunistically (with permission if it doesn't belong to you!). See Resources section for a good supplier of wildflower seed.

If you're growing a garden in which you will hold your wedding reception, and you desire an instant meadow for the event, then you might think about scraping off the top layer of soil and sowing wildflower seed. A cornfield mix is a quick-flowering mix of annuals which ought to shoot and flower on raked ground without too much difficulty, and is generally sown to flower in early summer. However, while easy, cornfield mixes can be a bit hit-and-miss, if you're looking for a perfect carpet of wildflowers to frame your day. You could cheat, if your budget allows. You can buy wildflower-seeded meadow grass matting, which you roll out on to the earth to grow into an instant meadow. We used these once to make meadow runners down the middle of the tables at a wedding reception, though I will admit that the stress involved in having the meadow in full flower and perfectly good condition in time for the wedding is not something I'd like to repeat.

What to grow

Well, with time and planning, you have a really wide choice of flowers to grow for an early-summer wedding. As I mention in other chapters, the skill is to edit the choice of what you'll grow to a tight five to seven different varieties. These will create the background, the base, in which those few roses or peonies can shine. Choose varieties that will work hard for you, to fill a gap in case there is one. Think about the shapes of bouquets and posies, and plant so that you have the necessary variety (accent flowers, daisy shapes, lace caps . . .) to make those shapes (see Chapter 1, page 29).

A bride's bouquet with roses, a foxglove, sweet peas, ammi majus, annual chrysanthemums, feverfew and achillea.

Hardy annuals

Direct-sow some hardy annuals in the autumn and another crop in early spring, and the autumn-sown ones will be flowering well for an early-summer wedding, with the spring-sown ready to take over if you've had a warm spring and the autumn-sown flowers are starting to look tired. See page 94 for more details.

Your plants will need feeding and staking (see Chapter 2, pages 38-41), and don't forget that they'll also need cutting! Annuals have one desire in life: to set seed. After

The hardy annual orlaya growing through pea netting arranged horizontally as support across a bed.

this they will die. Your challenge is to stop them setting seed – at least until after your wedding day. So as soon as they start flowering, no matter when your wedding date, you must start cutting the flowers they're producing. The more you cut, the more flowers you'll get.

The flowers you cut can be used to practise making posies and bouquets (see 'How to make a hand-tied posy or bouquet', page 162). The more you practise, the better you'll be prepared for the amount of flowers you'll need to create your dream, and the faster you'll get at making posies. You may think "Oh, we'll just have lots of posies dotted about the place," but practising making them will focus your mind, and you'll quickly realize that it's worth deciding how many posies you'll have, so that you know how many flowers to cut and how long it's going to take to make them.

Which hardy annuals to grow?

There are so many hardy annuals available to cut-flower growers that I could write a whole book about them alone. So here, as an example, I'm giving a short list of those I would grow if I were growing for my wedding. I'm remembering that I'm looking for flowers to do specific jobs in my mix: I need lace, spikes, greenery, scent, and flowers that won't wilt in buttonholes. I know that there'll be roses and peonies that I can cut from established gardens, so essentially my hardy annuals are to provide filler. Personally, for an early-summer date I would certainly grow more sweet peas than anything else – but that's because they're my favourite cut flower of all.

Take time to trawl through the good seed catalogues, whether on paper or online (see Resources section for recommendations). Read the growing tips, look at what the seed suppliers recommend, and choose flowers that work well together, as well as making an interesting mix of textures and shapes. The choice is wide, so give yourself plenty of time to think about it before you make any decisions.

Ammi majus

With its large, frothy, lacy white flower heads, ammi majus can be used as a frothy lace edging to larger, accent flowers; is useful as filler in posies and bouquets; and can equally be used as a stand-alone flower massed in a jug or perhaps a milk churn. We sow it in fortnightly batches from early spring onwards, in order to ensure a long season filled with ammi froth. It can be wilty if cut when the flowers aren't fully out, so be prepared to give it a good, long condition in water overnight before using it in floristry.

Bupleurum

This provides useful greenery to make a good understorey for your bouquets and posies, especially useful to grow if you have no alchemilla to hand. The lovely acid-green of the leaves and miniature flowers will add a bit of zing to your floristry. It will seed itself all over your garden if you let it, so, once you've grown it for your wedding, you may find you have it for years to come. Look for different varieties – a bronzy leaf, or a more acid-yellow flower.

Clary sage

These lovely spikes of coloured leaf bracts are available in white, blue and pink. The spikes grow beautifully tall, so the flowers are useful for height in bigger arrangements, as well as for backing in buttonholes, or to stop a bouquet having too smooth and life-less a dome to it. Very happy growing in a hot, dry patch.

Cornflowers

With small, dense flower heads in pink, white or blue, cornflowers bloom prolifi-cally. They are good for buttonholes and flower crowns, because they don't wilt, as well as for fresh petal confetti (see page 187). They are small-headed and fiddly to pick, though, so I'd say have some, but don't sow masses and masses and expect the flowers to fill a great deal of space. They are easy as pie to grow, though, and very satisfying for a new grower.

Nigella papillosa 'African Bride' – a gorgeous, strong, white variety. Sow a patch in autumn and a patch in late winter, and you'll have a good supply in early summer.

Nigella

The classic tall blue *Nigella damascena* (love-in-a-mist) is called 'Miss Jekyll', or you could try the white *Nigella papillosa* 'African Bride', with its large sprays of sharply dissected foliage. The flowers also make dramatic seedheads, which are useful in floristry too. Nigella isn't a wilty flower either, so it too is useful for flower crowns and buttonholes.

Sweet peas

Sweet peas earn a special place here, and not only because they're my favourite flower. I'd imagine that one of the reasons you might want to grow your own wedding flowers in the first place, if you're being married in the summer, is because you can then have a plentiful crop of sweet peas with which to scent and dress your wedding. Their scent, their frilly crêpe de Chine petals, the huge range of colours available, and the fact that they're very easy to grow, make them an obvious choice. Buying sweet peas at market can be difficult: they may not be fresh enough, and may have been treated with silver nitrate to stop them going over quickly, which will stop their wonderful scent.

Sweet peas can be massed on their own, or used as scented frilly filler in bouquets and posies. I think they're so wonderful that you could grow nothing but sweet peas for your wedding, and just have them massed in bowls and jugs about the place. However, if you're a beginner gardener, I wouldn't advise planning a sweet-pea-only wedding scheme, because if for any reason they fail, you won't have back-up. If you find that

Sweet pea 'Mollie Rilstone' – perfect for a ballet-shoe-pink scheme.

your sweet-pea crop is spectacularly in flower in time for your wedding, *then* you could have just armfuls of sweet peas about the place, and nothing else. But even then, if you have a lovely crop of ammi majus, some roses, sweet Williams and alchemilla, I'll bet you want to mix them up, at least in your bride's and bridesmaids' bouquets.

People often do buy a mass of sweet peas from me to have posied in jam jars down the dining tables at weddings, and it does look lovely and smell delicious to have that as a very simple scheme. If you're determined to have a sweet-pea-only scheme, then do look for a local grower who'll be prepared to supply you with some extra stems in case yours aren't in full flower yet. If you want to use jam jars, for sweet-pea-only posies on tables, you'll need about 15 stems per jar.

This is sweet pea 'Raspberry Ripple', an unusual red flake sweet pea, which I love mixed in with lots of other pink, white and red varieties.

A posy made up of mostly hardy annuals direct-sown the previous autumn.

The following are, I think, the best sweet peas for weddingy colours. They are all Spencer varieties, which have bigger heads and more heads per stem than the grandiflora or heritage varieties. Although the Spencers are less highly scented, they still have a scent to knock over your guests with its gorgeousness.

- 'Betty Maiden' – almost white, with a pale bluey-lilac edging
- 'Charlie's Angel' – a strong, pale lilac
- 'Daily Mail' – hot salmony pink: good for a stronger colour scheme
- 'Mollie Rilstone' – pale cream with ballet-shoe-pink edging
- 'Royal Wedding' – pure white.

When to sow your annuals

Early-summer weddings are lovely, but I recommend a bit of hedge-betting to ensure success in having all the annual flowers you've dreamed of. Unless you have very hard winters, then in early autumn the previous year, direct-sow half the patch you have at your disposal with a row each of your hardy annuals. You can thin those seedlings in the spring (winter may have thinned them enough for you in the meantime, so don't thin them in the autumn), when the little overwintered seedlings will begin to pounce into life. (The only flower I wouldn't direct-sow is the sweet pea, which is often the victim of a greedy mouse, and which I always sow in mouse-protected

Floristry tip

To arrange a selection of flowers in a shallow glass dish like this one, make a grid of narrow tape across the top of the vase and pop each stem, cut relatively short, into the spaces between the tape. This will prevent the heavy heads of the flowers from pulling themselves out of the vase.

A handful of about 20 sweet-pea stems arranged in a small pedestal vase.

This mix of early-summer flowers cut for a wedding includes sweet Williams and foxgloves. Foxgloves may well contort themselves into interesting shapes once cut. Do be careful with them: they are poisonous and you shouldn't let children handle them.

trays.) You can sow the same seed in seed trays, and again in late winter, to germinate under cover. This way, whatever the weather through winter and spring, you'll have success. See Chapter 2, pages 33-6, for further advice on seed sowing, including timing and spacing recommendations.

For the same reason – that you won't be able to guarantee your weather – and also an insurance in case you lose any seedlings to slugs, etc., it pays to also sow successionally in the spring: several times, 3 or 4 weeks apart. This way you can be sure to have flowers in bloom at exactly the right time for your wedding.

Biennials

Sown as seed the previous summer, biennials start to flower in late spring. So if you're to be married in late spring or early summer, and you know your date a year in advance, then you'll have time to pop in some sweet Williams, sweet rocket and foxgloves, say, for your big day.

Sow in seed trays in early summer, prick out the seedlings into individual pots when they're big enough to handle, and plant out in their flowering position in early autumn.

I've listed the following three biennials here because they're my favourites, but you

Foxglove 'Sutton's Apricot' is one of my absolute favourites and a lovely bridal colour – ballet-shoe pink.

broadcasting the seed into the ground and making the most of what comes up. I prefer to be a little more certain, and while it's really difficult to sow foxglove seed thinly enough in trays, when the seed does germinate, the seedlings are tough enough to be pricked out quite early, and they'll then grow on into sturdy little plants ready for tucking into the ground in their flowering positions in the autumn.

If you're growing a garden in which to hold your wedding reception, as well as flowers for the arrangements, then foxgloves give your borders great height and structure for early summer. And if you cut the tall stems for floristry, then they'll carry on flowering for you on side shoots for several months. Remember that foxgloves take a lot of space on the ground, so don't crowd them in with other flowers, or the others risk being mulched out of existence by the foxgloves' large, heavy, flat leaves.

could equally include wallflowers or Icelandic poppies, for example. Even parsley makes a lovely biennial cut flower, with gorgeous lemon-yellow umbellifer flower heads.

Foxgloves

These make great cut flowers, with height and bells to suit any colour scheme. I love 'Pam's Choice', white with dark pink freckles inside it; or 'Sutton's Apricot', a gorgeous pale peach, very fresh in a spring colour mix. Foxglove seed is arguably the smallest I'll sow in any year, and Ann, who works with us, swears that you're always better off

Sweet rocket

One of my favourite garden flowers, sweet rocket sports tall stems with sweetly scented white or lilac-coloured flowers bunched at the top. The flowering stems are a similar shape to lilac, or phlox, or paniculate hydrangeas. Sweet rocket will shoot more delicate flowers from smaller side stems and keep flowering for months. If it likes your soil, it will self-seed happily about the place and you'll have it popping up for years, reminding you, when it flowers, of the happy time when you were married. For weddings; for parties; for every day – a garden with sweet rocket flowering in it is a happy place.

Sweet William 'Auricula-Eyed Mixed' will give you lots of different colours, including this gorgeous deep pink.

Sweet Williams

Foxgloves give you spikes of height, sweet rocket gives you frothy lilac shapes, but sweet William gives you lovely plates of gently scented flowers on good strong stems that will last 2 weeks in water. Sweet William gives great bang for your buck, because the flower heads take up lots of space in floristry, so if you're looking for something that will really fill your arrangements and perhaps help you keep your overall stem-count down, then home-grown sweet William is the perfect choice.

Top tips for early-summer wedding flowers

✿ However tempting the endless choice of annuals you could grow, try to keep the number of types of flower you sow down to about five or seven: this will give your bouquets and posies a consistent 'look' (as well as making it easier when it comes to counting the stems you need to cut).

✿ Direct-sow half your seed in the ground in autumn, and sow the rest in trays under cover in late winter. This way you hedge your bets and can beat the weather, whatever it throws at you.

✿ But never sow sweet-pea seed direct into the ground! Mice love to eat the seed, so sow it in deep trays, and keep it protected from mice until the seedlings are well established.

✿ Remember that sappy early-season growth may look wilty when you cut it. Give your material plenty of time to condition in a cool, airy place out of direct sunlight, and it should bounce back nicely.

✿ If you know your wedding date at least a year in advance, do sow some biennial seed: early summer is *the* time for biennials, and they offer some gorgeous shapes and colours to use in your floristry.

AN EARLY-SUMMER WEDDING IN AN ELIZABETHAN MANOR HOUSE

The venue for this event was an old, old house in Gloucestershire. We used the structures the house and garden gave us for inspiration for hanging flowers and garlands, and we imagined the flowers against the colour of the stone. We used Victorian preserving jars (grand jam jars!) for masses of little posies about the place.

The ceremony was held in the dark, panelled hall of the house, and afterwards the guests were invited to a reception in a marquee on the lawn. All the posies were moved from the ceremony to the tables in the marquee, and the larger arrangements were moved to frame the marquee entrance and dress the buffet tables. So all the flowers were used twice, except for the garlanding and the heart. Even the bride's bouquet and the bridesmaids' posies were used after the ceremony to dress the cake table. Nothing went to waste. The whole event was bursting with flowers. Think about where you might be able to save time and use flowers to double up: it looks lovely after a ceremony if all the guests pick up posies and carry them to the reception venue – as though every guest is carrying a bunch of flowers.

This arrangement was made for the registrar's table: long and low, in a vintage, creamware vase, the stems are popped into a grid of tape. This stops the flowers falling over and means there's no need for flower foam.

A grand venue like this one can have its gates garlanded, but more modest arrangements on gates and entrances – a jar hanging on a door knocker, a scattering of rose petals leading up a path – can be just as effective.

For a stunning focal piece, keep an eye out for a good, heavy, pedestal container – this one is a cast-iron urn which was once painted white. The arrangement is made in a pot inside the urn, with a ball of chicken wire taped firmly inside the pot to give support to the tall stems.

Here's a Victorian preserving jar with a pretty posy in it, tied to the newel post of the staircase down which the bride made her grand entrance. After the ceremony the jar was untied and moved to dress one of the tables in the reception marquee. Waste not want not!

The bride's bouquet was made with the strongest-coloured flowers from the patch, so that it stood out from all the other flowers. After the ceremony (and having survived being chucked into the crowd and caught by a 10-year-old boy who dropped it!), it was put in a vase of water to dress the cake table.

Group small posies together to make more of an impact. Here they are edging a stone path leading to the ceremony.

That grand focal arrangement is now placed on a glass stand (actually an upturned giant vase) so that it looks incredibly light and airy against the dark old panelling.

This is a gigantic heart made of chicken wire, bound in a greenery garland and then dressed with roses and other goodies. The flowers were arranged first in small cushions of flower foam, then wired on to the garland. A project if you have a lot of confident flowery friends to help!

A little garlanding at a wedding goes a very long way. Garland entrances, pergolas, the top table . . . it is fiddly and time-consuming, but worth doing if you have time, material, and a team of helpers to install the garlanding at the last minute. See page 179 for garlanding instructions.

CHAPTER SIX

A HIGH SUMMER WEDDING

The height of summer is a glorious time to be married. The light intensity is more bleaching than in the paler, spring months, and the flowers that are in bloom at this time seem to be stronger in colour to compete with the light. High summer is definitely a time of year to think carefully about your colour scheme. Dahlias, sunflowers, zinnias, bells of Ireland, cosmos . . . choose jewel colours to go with this time of year. Of course, if your dream is for whites and pale pinks or blues, then you must grow those colours. But do bear in mind that the high-summer sun can create a sky of blank, blinding, colour-draining light.

These bright-coloured buttonholes are all together in a plastic takeaway container, having a nice drink until they're needed tomorrow. The yellow bobbles are craspedia – a great high-summer-flowering annual.

This mix is for a cheery, vintage-style wedding with jugs and jars and lively hand-tied posies. Yellow lifts a scheme – see how the yellow highlights stop the pinks and purples from being too blue.

White and pastel-coloured flowers can disappear in such tough conditions – especially if you plan to hold your ceremony and/or reception in an essentially white marquee.

Rich, jewel tones might be mixed into a paler base, for a bright effect to show up against white table napery or the sides of the marquee; even just against the sky. I recommend too that you look at yellow. (I hear intakes of breath from brides who'd never think of such a thing – though why yellow has such bad press in floristry I just don't know!) Sunflowers, for example, may not be to everybody's taste – though I adore them in wedding flowers – but do think of what they offer in colour. Even the palest bride at that time of year has good skin colour, and yellow is so sunny against happy, healthy, summer faces. And for those with really dark skins, rich, summer yellows sing like gold.

The colours may be glorious, but this can be a tough time to be growing for. Everything depends on the season you've had so far: an early spring or a hot, dry spell earlier in the season can mean that the flowers you've been growing so carefully have gone over. The skill with growing flowers for an event

This mix of jugs and jars, with sunflowers, dahlias and cosmos as the three main flowers, is all ready for an intimate wedding party. Just refresh the water in the morning and you're away.

at this time of year lies in late and successional sowing, and in watering and feeding. You don't need an enormous amount of stock to do your own wedding flowers, but you do need it to be in good condition. So sow annuals little and often, from mid spring until early summer, and you will have flowers to cut. And, depending on the season so far, you'll also have lots of greenery to use, from cutting the plants not yet in flower – or, alternatively, lovely seedheads from the flowers that have gone over already.

Hot weather at this time of year will put your flowers under pressure when it comes to cutting. Cut early in the morning or in the cool of the evening, into clean buckets of fresh water, and be sure to put them somewhere cool and airy to condition overnight before doing floristry with them. Be prepared to replace water in any glass containers on the day of the wedding, as in hot weather cut flowers can make the water dirty within hours.

What's in the garden already?

Hydrangeas. Here where we live, in the south-west of England, hydrangeas flower from the middle of summer until the first frosts: their wonderful, generous heads of flowers are a gift to the florist, from the opening of their first pale, waxy heads to those same flowers, slowly going over, maturing into richer colours – greens and purples and moody dark pinks. We can't grow them with enormous success here at Common Farm, because our clay is a little cold for them, no

A lace-capped hydrangea used as filler in a brides-maid's posy.

For information on how to make flower-foam-free centre-pieces like these, with hydrangeas and all the other goodies from your garden, see page 176.

matter how hard we work it. But world-class hydrangeas grow happily in the gardens of a neighbouring village only 3 miles away in Wiltshire, in what remains of the great Sel-wood Forest. I beg and borrow (but have yet to steal) hydrangeas from my friends up there, and use them in wedding schemes right up until early winter.

"But hydrangea flower heads are too big for my little posies!" I hear you cry. Cut them up; use them as filler. You don't have to use a whole hydrangea head at a time: a little goes a very long way.

They can be difficult to condition, especially early in their flowering season. The 'flowers' on the heads are actually leaves, and so can be wilty, especially if you cut hydrangeas from their woody, old-season stems. We cut hydrangeas early in the morning or late in the evening, stripping foliage straight off the stem before plunging the stems straight into buckets of clean water – a matter of seconds between the cutting and getting them into water. Plus we try to cut them only on their green (current season) stems, which are younger and have better spongy cellulose cells for the flower heads to drink up. (For

Buddleja flowers are even used here in tiny 'shot-glass posies', arranged in vintage glasses to mark the place settings on the top table at a wedding. If you make the top table the focus for all your floristry, then the photographs will be especially flowery, as most of the photographs of the day will be taken of you.

more on cutting and conditioning shrubby plants, see Chapter 3, page 45.) If hydrangeas really wilt, cut the stems again at a sharp angle, and lay them submerged in a bath of tepid water overnight. You'll be amazed! Once hydrangea flowers are past that very fresh, newly unfurled moment, and they begin to mature, you shouldn't have any problem conditioning them.

I will admit that I avoid using newly opened hydrangeas in flower-foam-based arrangements, as they don't last long, so for a high-summer wedding I might keep the flower foam at bay where hydrangeas are concerned. But once the flowers are fully open, or even beginning to dry out, then they're no longer so wilty, so I use them a great deal.

Other perennials and shrubs

Ordinary tree and hedgerow greenery can be beginning to look a little tired now. The fresh, zingy green of newly opened foliage

has been replaced as the leaves have grown heavier, thicker, a darker green. If you're growing your own, and have space, then bells of Ireland (see page 112) are a lighter, fresher green, so make a good alternative. Consider how much space you have. The alchemilla of the earlier summer will be over, but you could grow bupleurum to add that dash of bright green to your mix. Or, for silver-coloured foliage, try cineraria.

You could even use herbs for greenery. And herbs are often beginning to flower now: mints have pretty, brush-shaped flowers in pale mauves and purples – pineapple mint is especially useful, I think, with its variegated leaves and miniature buddleja-shaped flowers. They'll give scent to any bouquets that don't smell so sweet as the early-summer roses and lilac.

Buddleja, often known as the butterfly bush, is a favourite of mine for cutting. It is sometimes disparaged as a weed, but with good

Pineapple mint in a high-summer bride's bouquet. The scent is sharp and calming – good for a nervous bride.

These posies have a good, structural understorey of sedum in tight bud. Here at Common Farm, we cut sedum from the day the stems are long enough to be of any use until the end of the season, when we dry what remains for use in Christmas decorations. As with hydrangeas, very large heads can be split into more versatile smaller pieces.

management it will produce fine flowering shoots, which smell like honey. And, with one buddleja flower in your bouquet, you just might find yourself walking down the aisle with a butterfly to keep you company.

Echinacea flowers from high summer to the first frosts. Although the delicate petals are easy to bruise, these lovely flowers can give your arrangements a really wild, shaggy look, and their tall, strong stems are good for larger, wilder-looking arrangements.

Sedum makes a great filler at this time of year – it's a true workhorse in the cut-flower patch. From when the flower heads begin to bud up, in tight masses of silvery pinheads, to when the flowers open into great plates

of butterfly-beloved flowers, stems of sedum will give strength and understorey to your posies and bouquets. And remember, while the flowers may look as though they're too big to use in your floristry, they're all growing on short, individual stems, so you can split them to use as you like. Also, they don't wilt, so if you're thinking of making buttonholes or flower crowns, sedum cut as little sprigs will be useful in supporting other flowers.

As in any season, look around the gardens that are available to you. Depending on how the weather has been, there may be all sorts of unexpected offerings that I don't mention here. There are very few plants that won't condition well for cut-flower arrangements,

In this shot the bruised petals of a fully out echinacea flower have been removed, leaving only the bristling, thistle-like centre to the flower, a great piece of structural theatre in floristry. Just because a flower's no longer at its best doesn't mean it's useless ...

The nectar of a devil's bit scabious in the field, being drunk by a meadow brown butterfly.

so do play with unusual combinations. Your wild strawberry patch may be flowering, and wild strawberry flowers make beautiful buttons of daisy shapes in bouquets Even strawberries themselves are wonderful in floristry, though beware squashed strawberry juice on wedding dresses! (Better to use them before they're quite ripe.) If you are able to plan a whole year before your wedding date, look in the perennial beds for the highlights in your wedding flowers, and build your scheme around them.

Wildflowers

Wildflowers good for cutting are perhaps less prolific in the hedgerow at this time of year, but wild scabious varieties, like the ones we grow – devil's bit scabious and field scabious – and also the wonderful wild carrot, in flower throughout high summer, are easy to grow from seed. Both can be sown the previous summer, pricked out and planted out in early autumn, and will flower from the middle of summer the following

Bright annuals mixed in with roses make really beautiful high-summer wedding posies. The white, floppy daisy-shaped flower is Cosmos 'Purity'.

A bright bouquet with a few opportunistically cut roses framed by dahlias, ammi visnaga, wild carrot, zinnias and other goodies.

year. Wild carrot is a beautiful lace-headed umbellifer flower, tighter than cow parsley and ammi, with a tiny dot of very dark red at its centre. When the flowers are over, the developing seedheads are apple-green and strikingly architectural; we grow it in abundance, and it's one of my favourite flowers to cut through the summer.

What to grow

Well, the roses are more or less over until their second flush in early autumn, so don't rely on them for the wow factor in your wedding flowers at this time of year. There will be *some* roses, so you could still use them perhaps in your bridal bouquet and for the bridesmaids – but think, when planning, about other flowers that might be more reliable for you.

Remember that it's useful to have certain shapes to bring your bouquets and posies to life. The list I give on the following pages is by no means prescriptive, but it's designed to help you think about what you will grow. You might like the whole of your wedding to be just one shape, massed, in which case you must plant accordingly – though that way you're not giving yourself much space for creativity with whatever does best for you in your season.

Think spikes, daisy shapes, accent flowers, lace caps and buttons. For a high-summer wedding these could be (in the same order) larkspur or bells of Ireland, cosmos or zinnias, dahlias or sunflowers, ammi majus or ammi visnaga, and cornflowers, scabious or craspedia.

Bells of Ireland

These spikes of tall green flowers are brilliant as a green foil for whatever your colour scheme. At this time of year greenery can be difficult to come by, so grow some in the form of this sturdy, tall annual flower, and it'll do all sorts of jobs for you in your floristry. They flower on and on from side shoots, but will need feeding and watering to keep mildew and rust at bay if you're planning to use them late into autumn. They can have little, surprising sharp spikes tucked

The high-summer flowers bells of Ireland, buddleja and cosmos are all used in this jugs-and-jars, blue-and-white wedding scheme.

Cosmos is stronger-stemmed than it looks, which makes it very useful in giving life and movement to larger arrangements like this one.

underneath the flowers – which don't hurt particularly, but they do feel a bit savage when you first come across them.

Cosmos

This is *the* daisy shape for the high-summer or late-summer wedding. It's tender, so don't sow seed until mid spring, and then you can sow it direct in the ground. Cover it if there's a threatened frost, and you should have a good crop for your high-summer wedding. (By mid spring I'd really recommend you try to sow everything straight in the ground, just to save yourself time!) Remember how large these plants will get when fully grown – over 1m (about 4') each way, bigger than you

might think when holding a little spike of cosmos seed in your hand! – so give them space. Crowded annuals won't just fight for space above ground, their roots will also fight for water resources underground, and for a high-summer wedding you're asking flowers to perform in sometimes difficult conditions (hot and dry).

Keep an eye on the weather, and, while I don't generally advocate watering too much, if there's been no noticeable rain for a week or more then give your cosmos a really good water: you want the flowers to be large and generous and not spotted with botrytis, and the leaves not grey with mildew. A fortnightly feed with a weak seaweed solution will help too.

Dahlias

Dahlias start flowering soon after midsummer, and they flower on and on until the first frosts. They are not necessarily the first flower you may think of for a wedding – but for those of you who haven't yet been bitten by the dahlia bug, this may be your moment. No longer the private domain of obsessive allotmenteer gentlemen who grow them in frightening sizes and colours for the show bench, dahlias have danced out of competition halls and into the jam jars on wedding reception tables, welcomed with open arms by wedding flower designers.

They come in so many shapes and sizes and every single colour of the rainbow: from tiny pompoms, just right for a buttonhole, to huge dinner-plate dahlias big enough to wear as a hat, like 'Café au Lait' – much beloved of brides for its soft, creamy tones.

Dahlia 'Apricot Desire' is a favourite of mine: not too pink, with just enough ballet-shoe in it to make the colour interesting.

Dahlia 'Karma Fuchsiana' flowering in the field. This is a really gorgeous blinding pink, perfect for a flower scheme in very bright sunshine.

Then there are the gorgeous waterlily types like 'Apricot Desire', one of my favourites. I love the pinks and purples, the dark reds and the apricot dahlias. For me, dahlias are the cancan dancers of the cut-flower summer, and they should be dressed accordingly in jewel colours for their show.

Order dahlia tubers in the autumn from good suppliers (see Resources section). The more time you have to plan this, the more likely you are to get the dahlias you really want, so sit down and trawl through those websites. You'll need maybe six to ten dahlia plants if they are to be a central theme in your wedding flowers. You could choose ten different varieties to grow, but I'd be a little more circumspect and go for perhaps three plants of three different varieties. This will give your bouquets and posies a consistency that will help you achieve your wedding flower 'look'.

Growing your dahlias

The tubers will arrive as rooted cuttings in spring, and you should pot them up straight away in compost cut with plenty of sharp sand or horticultural grit: dahlias hate damp, and you don't want your newly arrived cuttings to damp off before they've even settled in a pot! Keep the pots somewhere frost-free (a greenhouse or polytunnel) until all risk of frost is past, and water sparingly. You might find that they grow so fast they need potting on once before you plant them out (look for

Massed dahlias in a bouquet are outrageous. You may not have enough to be so flagrant in all your posies, but for a bride's bouquet . . . I dare you!

Plant dahlias out into good, free-draining soil (again, we add a great deal of grit to our soil to stop our dahlia tubers suffering from damp) and feed them regularly: first with nettle tea to encourage stem growth, then, after midsummer, with comfrey tea to encourage flowering (see Chapter 2, page 38, for more on feeding). If you don't fancy getting into making home-made teas, then feed your dahlias every fortnight or so, from when you've planted them out, with very dilute seaweed solution, which will ensure you have large, healthy, many-flowered plants.

As the dahlia grows, do pinch out the first flowering tips: this will encourage side shoots and so a greater number of flowers for you to have for your wedding. Then, once it begins to flower, cut, cut and cut the flowers, to encourage further flowering. Never leave flowers on a plant and expect the plant to keep flowering – it won't, until the existing flower has been taken. So remove the flowers, practise making posies with them, and enjoy them – and you will have lots of flowers for your wedding. Dahlias will also need staking to support their brittle stems during summer storms (see Chapter 2, page 41).

Cutting and conditioning dahlias

In high summer the weather can be hot! So cut dahlias early in the morning, when the water is high in their necks after a long, cool night. Cut them when they're not fully out, and cut straight into water. Give them a good 12 hours to condition before using them in floristry, and they'll stand well for you. If using dahlias in glass vases, be prepared to change the water the day of the wedding.

roots curling out of the bottom of the pot to tell whether this is necessary). Dahlias are top of the list where greedy slugs are concerned, so keep the rims of your potted-up dahlias smeared all around with Vaseline – a barrier the slug will not cross. Shake salt to stick to the Vaseline, and you've got a double slug barrier.

Do not on any account give in to temptation and plant your dahlias out before all threat of frost is past. They'll probably survive a late frost, but the biting they get from it will leave them, and you, feeling despondent, and they may take a while to recover.

You will probably have arranged the flowers the day before and the water they're in will very likely have gone an unsightly yellow (dahlias do this to water). Change the water in the vases on the morning of the wedding, and you'll refresh the dahlias as well as have clean water sparkling in glass in your 'tablescapes'.

Sunflowers

Sunflowers make wonderful cut flowers, and there are so many different-coloured varieties, from the lovely dark mix of chocolates and rich red colours in 'Earth Walker' to the delicate, lemon-yellow 'Key Lime Pie'. We grow sunflowers especially because they are such good food for bees and other insects: in a garden you may not notice that

Sunflowers tend to face outwards rather than upwards – their name in French is *tournesol,* which means they turn to face the sun – and this can make it difficult to use them in floristry. The skill is to avoid fighting with them, and let them be the side of bouquets, rather than at the top.

the surface of the flower is covered in pollen, because the bees mow the flowers efficiently. Bring them indoors, however, and it's a different story.

So if you're planning to carry them in your bouquet, you may want to either decide that you won't worry about pollen on your dress, or you could grow 'allergy friendly' varieties. These will be F1 hybrids, which won't reproduce (or make pollen). Personally, I'd rather feed the bees and not worry about my dress . . . After all, one of the many good things about growing your own wedding flowers is that you're not just cancelling the carbon footprint of the flowers you have at your wedding, but you're actively feeding your environment by growing them in the first place.

Growing your sunflowers

I find sunflowers much easier to grow when they're direct-sown into warm ground in late spring. Then they germinate and grow on quickly. Sunflowers grown in pots, which then need potting on and planting out, will be fine, but may sulk a little when planted out, which can be unnerving for a novice grower. Of course, sunflower seed, direct-sown into the ground, can be a strong draw for the local hungry mouse – and, as the seed begins to sprout leaves, you do risk losing them to slugs. So, as usual, I recommend that you hedge your bets. Sow a couple of short rows of sunflowers in the ground, and put another ten seeds into pots. If your ground-sown seed takes, survives early mouse and slug attack, and starts shooting up quickly, then you can give away the seedlings you've got coming on in pots.

In the same way that a touch of yellow in a pink-and-white scheme can prevent that scheme from being too blue, a touch of pink in a yellow-and-white scheme gives the whole a gentleness. People don't like yellow because they think it's harsh – but not here.

When planting out sunflower seedlings, I recommend you do it early in the morning, when the sun isn't hot on the sunflower's head. Make sure you water them in very well, and maybe rig up a little shade in which they can recover from the trauma of transplanting. They will very likely look a bit wilty, but hold your nerve, water them every day until they stop sulking (a few days), and all will be well.

Pinch out the growing tips of sunflower plants as the first flowers show in bud, and you'll find you get lots of wonderful flowering side shoots, at a height you can reach, and that the flowers on those shoots are less heavy. These will be more useful in floristry than huge, prize-winning 20-foot-high flowers.

Sunflowers can sulk when they're cut as well as when they're planted out. Cut them early in the morning, straight into water, give them 12 hours in a cool, dark, airy place, and they'll recover beautifully. If you've practised cutting and creating your posies in advance, you won't be fazed by their moody behaviour when you cut them for the big day.

Zinnias

I first saw zinnias massed in northern India, at the very beginnings of the foothills of the Himalayas, in an area where the fields were full of apple trees. The nights there were cool; the days sunny. When I moved to Somerset,

One of the many good things about growing your own wedding flowers is that you're not just cancelling the carbon footprint of the flowers you have at your wedding, but you're actively feeding your environment by growing them in the first place.

This creamy-greeny-white zinnia is useful in all kinds of colour schemes. If you need stem length, look for the Benary's Giant series, which will give you more height than the bedding-style varieties, though these are still tall enough for posies, and easier to find in catalogues.

fussy. But for their happy, sunny faces in all those gorgeous colours, I will put myself to some trouble.

It is the perfectly matt, almost dusty surface of their velvet petals that I like so much. Their texture is a great foil for the dahlias and bouncy jolly cosmos also flowering at the same time. Direct-sow zinnias, after all threat of frost is past, and they'll do much better for you than grown in a tray then pricked and potted out, which disturbs their roots and upsets them.

Catch crops

Remember that you can pop in catch crops (quick-growing space fillers) of other annuals too, to dress the tables at your wedding. If you love cornflowers, gypsophila, California poppies or nigella, sow them late and they'll flower late for you. A tray of sweet peas sown in spring will flower from high summer onwards.

where the fields are full of apple trees and the nights are cool, and the days are (relatively) sunny, I determined that I would grow masses and masses of zinnias. I will admit, though, that they've been trickier to master as a crop than I anticipated. They like it really hot and dry. And they don't like their roots being disturbed once they've germinated. In short, they're a little bit

The skill with getting and keeping annuals in top condition for a high-summer or late-summer wedding is in feeding, watering and cutting. Don't let them dry out, or they'll go to seed. Keep them fed to keep

The skill with keeping annuals in top condition for a high-summer or late-summer wedding is in feeding, watering and cutting. Don't let them dry out, or they'll go to seed. Keep them fed to keep the flowering stems strong, and *cut* them, and they'll flower again.

A moody late-summer mix of late-sown (mid-spring) sweet peas, Japanese anemones, and black elder leaves.

the flowering stems strong, and *cut* them: don't expect flower heads to stay fresh on the plant for long in high summer. Annuals are cut-and-come-again flowers – so remember to cut them, and they'll flower for you again.

Top tips for high-summer wedding flowers

- Successional sowing is the key to having lots of flowery material to cut at this time of year. Sow one batch of flowers in early spring, another in mid spring, and another in late spring.

- Feed with weak seaweed solution and water often, to keep flowers producing and prevent them going to seed.

- Be ready for hot weather putting your cut flowers under pressure. Cut them early in the morning or in the cool of the evening, and put them somewhere cool and airy overnight. Replace water in jam jars and any other glass containers on the day of the wedding, if it has yellowed overnight.

- If flowers are starting to go over, don't ignore attractive seedheads: cut them and use them in your floristry.

- If cutting hydrangeas for a high-summer wedding, you'll find that as the flower heads mature they are easier to condition. Freshly opened hydrangea heads will do better in water than in flower-foam arrangements.

A COUNTRY WEDDING AT THE HEIGHT OF SUMMER

These pictures are from an orchard wedding reception in the bride's family's garden. The bride and groom skipped off to the registrar in the morning and were married with only their parents and brothers and sisters as witnesses. In the afternoon they had a small group of friends to a gorgeous party in the orchard at the bottom of their garden. The bride was brave (and clever) with her colour scheme, and the pale pink wine in the glasses provided a very successful contrast with the flowers. This was one of my favourite events of the year.

The bride asked for a ball of flowers to hang from the oak tree over the tables. This takes more material than you might think, but is fun to do and looks brilliant.

Extra buttonholes were popped into small, square jars around the tables. They were pinned at the back, so that people could wear them if they liked.

This is a loosely arranged jam-jar posy, with about 12 flower stems just popped into the jar. You need more stems to make a little hand-tied posy – which I prefer, because it looks more luxurious as well as being easier to transport.

A posy hung on a gate showed the guests which way to go to find the party.

This is a jam-jar posy which has been tied. It uses more stems, and is more luxurious looking, than the loosely arranged stems shown on the previous page. I like this version – but you must do what you wish!

The groom's buttonhole posy, with one white sweet pea, a yellow rudbeckia, and underneath it all a tiny supporting ledge of ammi visnaga.

The bride's bouquet had cream satin ribbon and also a lovely salmon-pink grosgrain ribbon, reflecting some of the colours in the flowers – and the colour of the wine.

The bride's bouquet was put in a vase to keep it fresh during the festivities. The colours of the flowers were bright, the orchard was beautiful, and so the couple sensibly stuck to plain white napery for their scheme.

CHAPTER SEVEN

AN AUTUMN WEDDING

Season of mists . . . apples, dahlias, fiery-coloured leaves, berries . . . This is a great time to be married if you love the rich, warm colours of autumn. Be warned, however, if you want a lot of garden flowers: then you need to think back to when the first frosts bit last year, the year before, and for several years before that – and set your wedding for a date at least a good fortnight before then.

Choose a date before you usually get your first frost. Your garden flowers will keep performing until then.

Here the colours are rather an unexpected combination: this is what happens when you're making the most of what's left in the garden. Sunflowers will bloom late into the autumn from a late sowing in high summer, but they can begin to look pinched as the nights get cooler.

It is the foliage which makes this mix so stunning: the lemon-yellow leaves of the hornbeam contrasting beautifully with the dark red of the smoke tree.

Here at Common Farm in Somerset, we often get a ground frost in the second week in October. Until then I'm (relatively) confident that we'll have a mass of dahlias and other garden goodies for use in our floristry. After that, and there's a good chance that we'll have slim pickings. True, the garden usually gives us dahlias until just late autumn, but not in the profusion we have until the first frost, and a month before that they're often looking a little tired.

So, for an autumn wedding, think outside the box: think wreathing, think fruit, think foliage and seedheads. The flowers you have can be the highlights in a wild mix of foraged leaves, nuts and apples. This is a time to perhaps be less prescriptive, and more imaginative about the colours and flowers you choose for your wedding scheme.

What's in the garden already?

Well really it's the time for foliage to sing, rather than flowers. Do you have scarlet oak? Sweet gum? Maples? Will there be hawthorn berries and sloes; old man's beard? Are there silver pennies of honesty seedheads for you to tuck into your posies and bouquets?

Cutting and conditioning autumn foliage

With late-season tree and shrub foliage, the risk is more that they'll drop than that they'll wilt. You don't need to sear the stems as you do in earlier seasons, but keeping cut stems in water will help stop the leaves drying out and dropping. And if leaves do drop, don't worry: it's the season for falling leaves! Use coloured leaves to scatter about the tablescapes at your reception. They will add a lovely hue and will reflect the garden outside beautifully. Of course, seedheads and twigs need no water, but berries will need water if you intend them to keep their bright shininess for more than a day or so.

A seedhead scheme with fruit. Something to think about, or perhaps to inspire you, if you're thinking of an autumn wedding.

Remember the necessary stem-count described in Chapter 1: approximately 600 stems. So do you think you'll be able to make up a good third of your stem-count, or maybe a lot more than that, with foliage and seedheads?

Flowering perennials

As the summer comes to a close, deadhead and feed your flowering perennials to keep them producing flowers, and to prevent the appearance of unsightly rust or mildew. People often relax towards the end of summer and just watch their gardens go over, as is normal for the season. Keep your garden deadheaded and fed, and you may be surprised at how long your plants keep producing new shoots of glorious colour.

I recommend you make use of all the flowering perennials available to you. You don't

know when the first frost will strike, and unless you've been very careful to set your wedding date well in advance of any frost risk, the skill is to be not too fussy about your colour palette, and work with what you have. I find that this end-of-season floristry forces me to be really creative with my work, and, as a result, the arrangements I make are much more visually exciting than with the lovely, much-easier-to-create-with flowers of late spring and summer.

Do you have asters in the gardens you can cut from? These gorgeous autumn daisy shapes make a great filler for posies and bouquets. They flower until the first frosts – as do penstemons, and late-season persicarias. Scabious will already have flowered, but when they look very seedheady (in late

Late-season persicarias giving a flash of deep pinkish-red to a bouquet filled with the last of the ammi majus, hawthorn berries, dark red elder foliage . . .

Delphiniums in late autumn? Don't rely on them, but if they're there, use them!

summer), cut them back, give them a feed (chicken-poo pellets will work well), and they'll re-shoot for you. Even if they're not in full flower, budding scabious is very pretty in posies and buttonholes.

Equally, delphiniums often have a second flush through till the first frosts. At the time of writing, at the very end of autumn, we still have a few in our garden, and we're still cutting them, though I would use them only opportunistically in a wedding scheme: I wouldn't be brave enough to make them the focus of wedding flowers this late in the season. Cut them back after their first flowering, feed, water and hope for the best.

Achillea flowers on and on for us, right up until the first frosts. Achillea at Common Farm is often the favourite home for a late hatch of greenfly, but you can rub off the greenfly easily enough and still use the flower heads.

Wildflowers and berries

There are seedheads to be found all over the place at this time of year: wild carrot, hogweed (be careful cutting hogweed, as the spiny stems can cause a severe skin reaction, so wear gloves) and scabious seed-heads are all structural and interesting in

I find that this end-of-season floristry forces me to be really creative with my work, and, as a result, the arrangements I make are much more visually exciting than with the lovely, much-easier-to-create-with flowers of late spring and summer.

arrangements. Look also for hedgerow berries: hawthorn has a lovely rich red berry, blackthorn will be laden with sloes (though be careful here too, as it's very spiny), and there are blackberries and crab apples; wild dogwood berries and wild iris berries. Look at the wild spaces available to you more closely at this time of year – from a distance, it may appear that there's nothing to cut.

What to grow

Dahlias, chrysanthemums, late annuals, and late-flowering bulbs such as nerine lilies and schizostylis make for a deliciously rich-coloured look when mixed with turning autumn foliage, berries and fruit. As with any season for which you might be growing, take time to do a little research into what might do well for you in your growing conditions.

Chrysanthemums

No chapter on autumn weddings would be complete without mentioning this classic of the autumn border. Like dahlias, chrysanthemums are enjoying something of a resurgence in popularity, and people are discovering the gorgeous shapes and colours

you can grow. Banish their sometimes doleful reputation, and think instead of how they can give you a trusty understorey to your flowers. Use chrysanthemums to make structural shapes; for green flowers; for daisy sprays of little white blooms.

Order young, rooted cuttings early in the year from a reliable source (see Resources section) and pot them up when they arrive. You can find amazing displays of chrysanths at large horticultural shows, even early in the season. We bought our first collection when we saw them at the Malvern Show in late spring, and they flowered beautifully for us that autumn. If you have greenhouse or polytunnel space at your disposal once the weather starts to cool, I'd recommend keeping the young plants potted up (and fed and watered) outdoors through the summer months while they grow on, remembering to pinch out flowering tips as they appear, to encourage bushing up and lots of flowering stems. Then, when the temperature starts to drop, you can bring them under cover and they'll flower well into the late autumn.

If you don't have space under cover, then try to plant your chrysanthemums in a sheltered patch in the garden, not only to

This bride chose red and white for her late-autumn scheme, and the late-season chrysanthemums were very effective with schizostylis and other seasonal goodies.

prevent them being pinched by cold, but also to protect them from battering by wind. You want your wedding flowers to be perfect, not wind-lashed and weather-bruised.

Chrysanthemums will respond well to regular feeding with a weak seaweed solution. They can get powdery mildew in a wet spell, dry mildew if their roots dry out, leggy if not cut hard enough . . . they are, I find, a little fussy. (But then, they might not love it as much in our damp, dank autumn conditions here in Somerset as they might somewhere a little sunnier and drier.) We did use both red and white chrysanths in an unusual

autumn wedding scheme last year, and mixed with anemones, paperwhite narcissi, schizostylis and greenery they did look great – and the bride loved them. So do think about chrysanthemums for an autumn wedding: if you have a protected spot, it might be well worth trying some.

Dahlias

Dahlias will flower until the first sharp frost, after which they are not to be trusted. But, if your wedding date is before you're likely to have a proper frost, then do plan to use dahlias in your scheme. Their wild dancing

A late-autumn bouquet with dahlias and dark elder foliage.

This pedestal arrangement has late-season foliage, rich dark dahlias, pink cosmos, trails of amaranthus... An arrangement like this needs about 75 stems of foliage and flowers and could be used to frame the ceremony, then be moved to make a focal piece at the reception.

make them my second-favourite garden flower (after sweet peas, which stole my heart long before I'd ever even heard of the dahlia). Dahlias will start flowering from high summer, and to have them in tip-top condition for an autumn wedding you'll need to keep deadheading and feeding them fortnightly with a weak seaweed solution.

Order your dahlias from reputable suppliers, and they will arrive in mid spring as rooted cuttings. By the end of the season these tiny cuttings will have grown and grown to be nearly 1.5m (4-5') high, and 1m (3') wide, loaded with gorgeous, cuttable flowers.

See Chapter 6, page 114, for more on ordering and growing dahlias, but for an autumn wedding you might want to think differently about colour. As the year turns, the light seems to make the colours in each dahlia petal richer and more varied: a dark red dahlia in high summer may appear flat in colour, even bland, but by autumn those plain-coloured petals will have morphed into stripes you couldn't see before – more vibrant variations on a theme. So when you choose dahlias for your wedding, think of what will go well with your autumn foliage; with the fruit and nuts you might add in to the mix. Be imaginative. For the autumn-wed couple, growing your own wedding flowers offers the richest possibilities in wild colour combinations. Go on, I dare you!

Bulbs

Bulbs aren't just for spring: there is a good selection for flowers in autumn. They all take a while to clump up and make a really good show, but if you're growing them actually for your wedding, each bulb should give you at least one flower, so you can plan in advance for the number of stems you need. Nerines and schizostylis flower for a good, long time in the garden, and, unlike in the summer months, when a flower can go over in a matter of days when the sun is high on its head, autumn flowers should last longer on the plant. Ask your bulb supplier for specific advice on growing autumn bulbs (see Resources section for recommendations).

Acidanthera

An early-autumn flowerer, this white gladiolus with its dark-plum-coloured middle has a glorious, intense scent, which can be over-powering if you use too many of them in bouquets and posies for indoors. The bulbs are cheap, but not very hardy, so they're unlikely to overwinter well. Here in the relatively warm south-west of England, I plant acidanthera anew every year, as very few re-emerge each spring.

Plant in mid spring, in a hot, dry place, and enjoy the flowers when they come. They can be unreliable flowerers – ours didn't flower at all the year before last, and patchily this year, despite our buying bulbs from an extremely reliable supplier, so it's perhaps wise to not plan for acidanthera to play a major role in your wedding flowers. But just one, in your bride's bouquet, is heaven, and very unusual.

Crocosmia

After vibrant flowers through high-to-late summer, you're left with the most fantastic curving fronds of seedheads. Use them in taller arrangements, in jugs and baskets. Autumn is a time of rich pickings for seedheads, but crocosmia is one of my favourites.

Nerine lilies

The burst of pink from a nerine lily can be the theme colour for your scheme. I love the way these late-season flowers really take you by surprise, as they look like the sort of thing that would flower earlier in the year. But throughout the autumn you find these glorious pink lilies flourishing (in hot, protected, dry beds); bursting colour through the gloom. My own wedding bouquet was cut entirely from the garden and hedgerow one

This bouquet of the last dark dahlias has shoots of bright pink nerine lilies coming out in it. They'll stop the dark dahlias looking too gloomy in the late-season light.

morning in late autumn: my mother created a bouquet of one nerine lily, old man's beard, blackberries, purple dogwood leaves, acorns and oak leaves. I loved it, and wish I had a better photograph to share here, but I was very keen not to spend any money on my wedding (we needed to save every penny for Common Farm), and so didn't even have a photographer, other than family members taking happy snaps.

Paperwhite narcissi

Narcissi might be a surprising idea for an autumn wedding, but they will reward you with tiny scented stars just 6 weeks from planting. So when you're clearing space in early autumn, pop a hundred or so paper-

Early paperwhites in a scheme with the last of the opportunistically cut roses. An unusual mixture, and full of scent.

The schizostylis here is used for the fieriness of its pink when put with dark reds and oranges. With whites and paler tones, this little lily seems a gentler colour.

whites into the ground, and they'll be up and in flower for you in no time. They won't have enormously long stems, but they're perfect for posies, have a wonderful scent, and it's as though there's a magic wand of spring pinging up all over the place, taking away the threat of winter.

Schizostylis

These delicate shoots of redder pinks than nerines will grow in damp soil and clump up to make great little fronds of autumn colour. If you plant them in the spring of the very year of your wedding, you won't get many more flowers than the number of bulbs you plant, but if someone you know has some already established in their garden, then do beg them to allow you to cut them, as they add life and vibrancy to a late-season look.

Budgeting tip

The further you go from a big city, the less expensive your venue will be. Large country houses are increasingly available to hire from Friday to Sunday, and often have accommodation for up to 70 people. If you would rather celebrate with lots of friends than have lots of presents, you could ask guests to contribute to a country-house weekend instead of buying from a wedding list – giving you a Downton-type experience without a bank-breaking cost.

Annuals for a late-season show

To have annuals flowering in really good condition through the autumn you need to sow your seed late: that's high-summer late. For the usual summer show, it's counter-intuitive to be seeding ground so far into the season – but you're being clever, and planning for plants to be in first-class condition much later. Prepare your ground so that it's a clean, fine tilth, and sow your seed sparingly, as you would earlier in the season.

Now, your challenge is to get the flowers germinating, growing and flowering – and the trick is to water. This seed will germinate and try to flower very quickly, so it might not get its roots down so far in the search for water as its older sisters, sown in spring, would do. The summer months can be dry, and you're looking for quick germination and good growth before a late show of flowers. This year we sowed seed in the middle of summer and it flowered before the end of the season. If we'd watered it more (I am mean with water), we'd have got a better show, but we already had a good gardenful of flowers, and sowed so late really as an experiment. If you're sowing for a wedding, then you will doubtless take better care and pay more attention, and you'll get a better crop than we did.

Ammi visnaga

This stronger-stemmed ammi (than its cousin ammi majus) takes all summer to come to flower. You might want make a couple of little sowings, in order to ensure you'll have some. Sow the first batch at the end of spring, and the second a month later, in early summer. If you do sow in early summer (as I recommend for an autumn wedding), make sure to keep watering the seed after sowing, to encourage speedy germination and growth. I've been cutting an ammi visnaga crop sown in early summer this year since mid autumn, but it's a slow plant to get going, and I admit I've been cutting it before the flowers have ever properly come out. If I'd watered the seed more when I sowed it, I'd have more flowers now, as the seed would have sprouted more quickly.

"BRIDE OR GROOM?"

The bride stands on the left of the groom, and her family and guests behind her on the left, because in the olden days the groom would need to keep his sword hand free in case of attack, and his sword hand was more often his right hand than his left. The association of women with the left-hand side continues with the phrase 'the distaff line'. The distaff was the hand-held spinner used to spin thread for weaving, which women would habitually hold, when they weren't doing other chores, in their left hand, and so the distaff line means the maternal side of a family. In old family pictures women are generally seen standing on the left-hand side.

Bells of Ireland

This is great for an amazingly hardy late-season crop. Direct-sow the seed in early summer for an autumn flowering. I love the way it will keep on cropping from side shoots, which curl up strongly to take the place of early cutting. Bells of Ireland is an incredibly hard worker in the cut-flower patch, and in a season when there might be less greenery than you'd like, it's useful just for its colour as much as for its interesting structure and shape. It can suffer from mildew and rust if the roots are very dry, so do water through the hotter months – though, as the season closes, you might find you get enough rain to keep the rust at bay.

California poppies

Sown in early summer, California poppies will flower strongly in the autumn, giving you delicate additions to your bouquets and posies. The foliage is very pretty in bouquets too, although it can be brittle, so be careful when handling it. California poppies flower and go over in a heartbeat, so don't plan your whole scheme around them, but do make the most of these delicate flowers with their satin-skirt-panel petals when you can.

Cosmos

Providing an abundant source of big, daisy-shaped flowers, cosmos will flower until the first frosts. In all kinds of colours, from pure white to dark cranberry via yellow and orange and pink-edged white, with doubles and shell shapes to ring the changes as you go, cosmos is easy to grow and satisfying to cut. You could do a whole wedding scheme

Cosmos 'Purity' in a ball of flowers above a church porch.

with just cosmos in the early autumn. (However, I say never put all your eggs in one basket: the year you grow nothing else, your cosmos will of course suffer from some nasty blight; you'll find you've sown the wrong colour; it'll all get mildew . . .)

It's not all easy-peasy with cosmos, though. To have an abundance of flowers on your wedding day, you must cut the flowers from the day your cosmos starts flowering. And you must feed your plants: they'll get rust and mildew if you expect them to perform for months on end. And sow your seed late: in early summer rather than spring. Then your plants will start flowering in late summer rather than high summer and will be in good condition for cutting in autumn. You can't really expect annuals to keep producing big quantities of high-quality flowers for more than about 6 weeks, so sow your cosmos late and don't worry about not having any flowers in high summer, because you'll have lots for your big day.

This bride wanted bright bright bright autumn colours in her bouquet, and the perfect orange of this California poppy was just right for her.

Feverfew

Feverfew will flower right through to the first frosts. Sow seed in the ground in mid-summer for a late-season crop. Look at the lovely double feverfew 'Tetrawhite' as an alternative to the classic, simple, yellow-centred daisy shape. You may be using lots of seedheads and foliage in your arrangements, but you'll still need filler, and a little patch of feverfew will do this for you.

Late sunflowers

For the autumn wedding, so long as you indulge in a lot of careful watering and feeding through the summer, there's no reason why you can't have quite a lot of different annuals, including that stalwart of the high and late summer, the sunflower. The skill, as I've said throughout this chapter, is to sow your seed almost so late that you don't believe a single flower will come up. A neighbour of mine here in Somerset has had an incredible field of sunflowers this autumn, and the seed wasn't drilled in until mid July. While my ageing sunflower plants were collapsing under the weight of their many-times-cut-from trunks, their flowers dotted with botrytis and their stems grey with mildew, my neighbour's grew and budded up and flowered all through mid autumn, when I would have given my right arm for such a crop.

But, as I've been stressing throughout this book, with annuals there is no guarantee how quickly they'll flower, or how long they'll keep flowering before going over. So make a few sowings of sunflowers, two or three times over a period of perhaps 6 weeks, and you'll have lots for your wedding. For an autumn wedding, sow right at the start of summer, again in midsummer, and again a couple of weeks later, and do be sure to water the seed in well, to ensure speedy germination and strong growth.

You can pinch out the growing tips to encourage side shoots, which will give you more, if smaller, flower heads: you're growing for wedding flowers, so I doubt you'll be looking for one single half-metre-wide flower head when you could have many smaller blooms to use in your bouquets. See Chapter 6, page 116, for more advice on growing sunflowers.

Top tips for autumn wedding flowers

- Five reliable flowers I'd recommend for autumn are ammi visnaga, dahlias, chrysanthemums, nerine lilies and schizostylis.

- Beware the first frosts. If you'd like flowers for your wedding, you need to book a date before your garden is likely to freeze.

- Be opportunistic with autumn berries and seedheads. Take what the season offers you and make the most of it.

- Autumn foliage and berries will do better if conditioned in water than if not: berries lose their shine, shrivel up, and drop fairly quickly without water.

- Don't let your garden feel all end-of-seasony and let it go over. Keep the plants in your borders cut, fed and watered, and you'll be surprised how your flowering perennials go on giving.

AN AUTUMN WEDDING IN A SEASIDE VICTORIAN HOUSE

This wedding took place in a wonderful house on the north Somerset coast. The venue is a bit of a 'wedding factory', with different couples using it for their celebrations most days of the week, especially over the weekend. We couldn't deliver the flowers before 10am on the Saturday, and the ceremony itself was booked for 2pm. If you're planning on doing your own flowers in a hired venue, it's really important to check what time the venue will let you arrive. You won't have time to do much floristry on the day of the wedding itself, so keep the plan relatively simple, so you can manage the time you have easily. We did these flowers the day before the first frost, when all the dahlias were bitten off. Lucky bride! Note that there are roses in the mix as well as dahlias, blackberries, crab apples, and so on. We knew that the frost was coming, and so we cut everything in the garden to use for this bride's day.

We made the most of the last of the garden roses for the focal piece created for the registrar's ceremony table, which was then moved to the top table at the reception.

The groom, the ushers and the fathers of the bride and groom all had little bunches of crab apples as part of their buttonholes.

This generous jam-jar posy filled the centre of the table at the reception. The bride scattered pine cones and ivy leaves around the tables too, to finish her autumnal look.

The bride's bouquet was collared with bright foliage from a maple tree, and we used late clover foliage too, to give the bouquet a meadow feel.

The bride and bridesmaids too had crab apples in their bouquets and posies. Will you have fruit in the gardens you pick from, which you can use in your arrangements?

With the sun low, the light was strong in this glass-framed room, and the bright colours showed up well, whereas paler colours would have been bleached out.

CHAPTER EIGHT

A WINTER WEDDING

There are lots of reasons to be married in winter: you love the glow of candles in the dark; you've always wanted to wear velvet on your wedding day; you're saving up for a house, and the reception venue is a third of the price it is in summer . . . The important part is you and your betrothed standing up and declaring that you intend to make a life together. Everything else is framing – and a grow-your-own winter wedding can be one of the most beautiful and romantically framed days imaginable.

An arrangement of mostly foliage and foraged berries, with just a few greenhouse ranunculus and the addition of candles, makes a very effective table centrepiece.

A winter bride's bouquet with Cornish anemones, ranunculus and paperwhites, with ordinary garden ivy and berries, viburnum and other winter foliage.

You will have to abandon all thoughts of roses or peonies or dahlias, and focus on what can be grown through months with low, low light levels, and perhaps under cover. A greenhouse or polytunnel are useful tools for a winter wedding. But, for me, it is the exquisite dot of light in a painting that makes the image breathtaking, and so it will be for you in winter: windowsills garlanded with greenery and dotted with pillar candles; a bride's bouquet made entirely from hedgerow bounty, with perhaps just a few forced paperwhite narcissi, very early ranunculus or anemones you've grown in a warm greenhouse; or a handful of hellebores and lungwort framed with ivy berries and early shoots of honeysuckle. (If you want to use candles, do check in advance whether your venue allows open flames. And, of course, bear in mind fire risk when combining candles with dried plant material in arrangements.)

Base your winter wedding around foliage, with a deal of clever lighting, and you may not need to grow any flowers at all. With access to an ivy-hanging wood (permission granted of course), you could simply garland yourself, your intended, the tables and even your guests. Use stone, wood, moss and

A cushion of paperwhites in a pedestal glass vase is beautifully scented as well as enchanting to look at.

Hellebore tip

For cut hellebores to last in water, they need to have begun to set seed on the most open flower in the spray. Before then, hellebores will last only a matter of hours in water. Once the seed has begun to set they hold very well, even out of water, so make pretty additions to button-holes or flower crowns, or as single flowers tucked into the bride's hair.

for this time of year. Questions like "Where will the focus flower go?" are especially irrelevant now. Be clever and creative, and enjoy yourself. And, if you do find that you need more flowers than you're able to provide yourself, you should be able to find a local professional grower to supply winter flowers to supplement your own stock (see Resources section).

berries, and your wedding table centres can be made into beautiful miniature gardens. Of course, you could pot up scented narcissi to grow into table centrepieces – or dig up clumps of snowdrops and put them into cups and saucers for an unusual look. If your hellebores flower early (we have them from late winter onwards, here in south-west England), then they too can be used in your scheme.

Winter weddings are a time to use your initiative and be adventurous with the finds you make when foraging. It's no good look-ing at rule books when growing your own

Hellebores make wonderful flowers for winter arrange-ments, but wait until the seed pods are just beginning to set before using them, if you want the flowers to last.

What's in the garden already?

Evergreens, of course: pine, ivy, euonymus. Lichen-covered boughs, pussy willow, hazel catkins, dried hydrangea heads, grasses, winter-hardy perennial euphorbias (be careful when handling: see Chapter 3, page 47) . . . Avoid being too prescriptive about what each table centre must look like. Don't expect every pew-end to be exactly the same as its neighbour. This is *not* the season to be too matchy-matchy.

Perhaps surprisingly, winter-flowering shrubs offer some delectable scents: sweet box, winter-flowering viburnums, winter-flowering honeysuckle – all have tiny flowers with such an intense fragrance that a tiny sprig dotted into each bouquet or posy will scent the whole wedding venue. Rosemary too makes a lovely scented extra ingredient in winter wedding floristry. I'm often asked

to include a little rosemary in a wedding bouquet in memory of a beloved family member who has died, so it can give meaning as well as scent to your day.

Wild berries and seedheads

One of the early signs that I was going to take up flower farming for a living one day occurred at the offices of *American Vogue* in Paris, where I was working at the time. I was about 25 years old, and in deep awe of my boss, Susan Train, and so when people sent giant trays of macaroons, their whole new make-up collection, or bottles of champagne for her to try, I was never surprised: I'd have sent her these things too. But the best gift I think I ever saw was a huge, shallow basket filled only with ivy berries and very dark purple tulips (which I know now were probably 'Queen of Night'), sent to her by Karl Lagerfeld via the florist Moulié, around the corner from the office. The design was simple and extremely effective, and it was the ivy flowers that provided the bouncing life to the design, rather than the rather stiff – though stunning – tulips.

Your garden in winter is full of such life: flowering ivy berries; budding cones on pine boughs; sturdy leaves on evergreens; shiny black sloes and bright pink-and-orange spindle berries in the hedgerow; old man's beard still trailing along, just asking to be cut. When I teach floristry in the winter, people often say "But there's nothing in the garden at this time of year." People tend to stand near the back door, unwilling to go out into the cold unless they know their trip

Viburnum bodnantense has a gorgeous scent in winter.

Spindle berries bursting out of a winter bouquet: bright buttons of pink and orange colour lighting up the gloom.

This foraged winter bouquet of twigs, berries and coloured leaves is full of colour and texture.

will be rewarded, and they look at their garden from this distance, and see no enchanting detail. The photograph above isn't great (winter light is very hard to photograph in), but it shows a totally foraged posy, with twigs, leaves and berries. The ingredients, to give you an idea of what's possible, are as follows:

- hawthorn berries
- dogwood leaves (yellow)
- lichen-covered apple twig
- winter-flowering honeysuckle
- dried *Spiraea* x *billardii* heads
- wild iris seedheads
- hogweed seedheads
- willow
- rose hips.

What to grow

If you have a bit of greenhouse space, a warm tunnel, or even space in the house with good natural light, then you have room to force bulbs for a winter wedding, or have ranunculus and anemones flowering early. One year I grew a whole crop of amaryllis in mushroom crates in my warm, sunny bathroom – slightly invasive for the rest of my family, but I was pleased with the results.

Bulbs for forcing

There are all kinds of bulbs that will force nicely for a winter wedding. From huge-headed amaryllis to tiny, delicate snowdrops and crocuses, via gloriously scented hyacinths and delicious bobbing heads of paperwhite narcissi, you could easily build your winter wedding scheme around forced bulbs.

Order your bulbs from a reputable online supplier in the middle of summer (when they will have great stock and won't have run out of your choices). Tell the supplier when you'd like them delivered – if you don't, then you're likely to get the bulbs in high summer, which might be too early for your purposes. Also ask their advice about the best time to pot up the bulbs to have them ready for your wedding date. Bulb suppliers are full of useful knowledge and love to share their expertise, and you'll get much better information from them than from your local garden centre, which might be selling bulbs, but which will not necessarily have very expert sales assistants.

The delivery date for your bulbs is important, because it's better that they are kept in the bulb supplier's cool, damp-free storage, than that you have to try to create the optimum storage conditions until you're ready to plant them.

For forcing, make sure you order bulbs that have been 'prepared': this means that they've already been given a cold snap to trick them into thinking that winter is over, and you can pot them up and start growing them straight away.

You'll need to be able to heat your greenhouse a little, or be prepared to bring flowers inside the house to hurry them up – so plant in trays or pots that aren't so large they're too heavy to lift. You can move them in and

RAIN OR SHINE

In France the phrase "Un mariage pluvieux est un mariage heureux" translates as "A rainy wedding makes for a happy marriage".

Two bridesmaids await the start of the ceremony in the rain.

out of the warm in order to encourage quicker flowering or to slow the process down, depending on the weather or how hot your house is. In general, unless you need to hurry them up, keep potted bulbs in a frost-free environment, perhaps at about 12°C (54°F) or just above, to bring them on.

Bulbs for forcing need not be planted deeply. Narcissi, hyacinths and amaryllis can be placed so that half the bulb stands free of the surface of the compost. We make bulb-forcing compost using a mix of 50 per cent horticultural grit and 50 per cent municipal green-waste compost, which makes for good drainage. If you're growing a great many to cut, then you could think about using recycled mushroom-growing trays as growing containers.

If you've been clever and arranged for the bulbs to be delivered at just the right time for your plans, then you can pot them up as soon as they arrive (so long as they've been 'prepared'). To give you ball-park figures: amaryllis take about 12 weeks to flower, hyacinths about 9 weeks, and paperwhite narcissi as little as 6 weeks. I recommend with snowdrops that you dig them up from the garden when you see them shooting, and pot them up then. This way you'll have a good clump flowering. They have a delicious honey scent, which in the middle of winter is a proper treat.

Think about growing bulbs to display in their pots, as well as for cutting. You can use attractive and imaginative containers: from tea cups to vintage buckets; vases to trifle

A posy of forced narcissi and tulips with a gorgeous heart of winter-bright willow.

bowls. With some judiciously placed moss as a top dressing and perhaps some tall twigs to support weaker, forced stems, you could save yourself a lot of flower-arranging time by growing arrangements to be your table centrepieces as they are.

Amaryllis

Make sure the amaryllis bulbs you order are large and firm. If they arrive and feel squashy, send them back. They will benefit from being soaked for an hour in warm water before you pot them up, which will rehydrate them if they've been kept dry for a long time. Plant them individually in pots of well-drained potting compost, leaving the top half of the bulb standing proud of the surface. You could pot up a lot of amaryllis together, but the pot would be heavy to move in and out of warmth, which you need to do to make the flowers come when you need them.

In the past I have planted six bulbs to a mushroom compost tray. You may prefer to pot them up individually, in case you decide that you'll use the flowers, still growing in pots, as your table centrepieces. Like hyacinths (see opposite), amaryllis can be grown just with their roots in water. So you could fill a glass vase with attractive gravel and place the bulb on top of the gravel, filling with water to the top of the gravel, and grow them like that for table centrepieces.

Each bulb should give you up to three large flowering stalks, with up to three flowers on each stalk. Amaryllis can be frustrating to get to flower, and are an expensive option to grow yourself. If you find they're in full bud

Think about growing bulbs to display in their pots, as well as for cutting. You can use attractive and imaginative containers: from tea cups to vintage buckets; vases to trifle bowls.

but the buds aren't opening, you can cut them, about a week before the wedding, and fill the stems with warm water, then, keeping the stems full, hang them upside down (so that the warm water stays near the tight-shut flower heads) indoors. I can see you shaking your head, and thinking "Perhaps not amaryllis." But don't be put off. The flowers last for weeks and weeks when they're open, so work backwards from your wedding date to have your amaryllis in flower perhaps a week or 10 days before, and you'll be fine.

Crocuses

These pot up very prettily in attractive containers. A fellow farmer/florist, Tuckshop Flowers in Birmingham, pots them up in vintage china cups and saucers, which she forages from flea markets and charity shops throughout the year, and they are, I think, enchanting, and would make charming wedding table centrepieces. Plant your crocus bulbs 6-8 weeks before you want them to be in flower.

Hyacinths

I love the scent of hyacinths in the deep winter months, and their pure, zingy colours cheer even the dullest of dark days. Plant

Crocuses growing out of a stamped silver jug with a collection of tiny vases of forced anemones and a handful of foliage – striking, and requiring very little material.

them half proud of well-drained compost. In fact, no bulbs really need to grow in earth: they have all the goodness they need to grow in the bulb itself. You can grow them in just water – but if you do, you need to keep the roots in water and the bulb out of water, which is why it might be easier to

A pedestal vase with white hyacinths and winter greenery. Beautiful and scented on a dark day.

grow them in compost. You can get old-fashioned hyacinth vases, designed for the bulb to sit at the top with just enough water to touch the roots, and to grow with no compost at all (a great way for children to see the bulb-growing process in action).

Hyacinths can be short-stemmed, which makes them difficult to use as cut flowers. To use them cut in bouquets and posies, grow them somewhere where they'll have to reach for the light, for example under a table or sideboard.

Narcissi

There are lots of highly scented narcissi which can be forced to flower in winter. *Narcissus papyraceus* (the true paperwhite narcissus), 'Erlicheer' and 'Grand Soleil d'Or' are three reliable winter-flowering narcissi, easy to force in the house or greenhouse. (This sort of narcissi are all generally known as 'paperwhites'.) Buy them 'prepared', and check with your supplier how long each variety will need to be potted up for to bring it into flower. Most will be in flower about 6 weeks from planting, but there are varia-

I use scented narcissi in floristry throughout winter. These flowers are all grown in the UK, but not by me.

for good local suppliers of home-grown stock (see Resources section for recommendations), and you might find it's easier and not much more costly to order from them than to grow the flowers yourself for your winter wedding.

Snowdrops

Dig clumps of these out of the ground when you see the foliage appear (assuming you have permission – remember that in the UK it's illegal to dig up plants from the wild!) and pot them up. You'll see snowdrop foliage shooting only 2 or 3 weeks before they flower – they always catch me by surprise. I would be opportunistic with snowdrops for a wedding in the middle of winter: if you see them popping up, dig some up and pot them in attractive containers to flower for you. If you're ordering them as bulbs, they are usually sent out when ordered 'in the green', i.e. when they've just flowered the previous winter. You'll need to plant them in the ground and remember where they are to dig them up the next winter.

tions. Forced narcissi can get leggy, and their stems lacking in strength, from growing so tall and fast in the warm. So once you've planted them (just put a little of the bulb in the growing medium, they don't need much soil), add a frame of hazel twigs to support the stems as they grow up.

I use scented narcissi in floristry all through the winter. My Cornish colleagues grow millions of them, and I order them throughout the dark months to supplement my meagre garden stock. They never let me down. Look

Budgeting tip

eBay is wedding accessories central. A great many brides buy their accessories – from their dress to their candles, from the bows on their chairs to their bunting – on eBay. I had one bride whose dress was then back on eBay by the end of the wedding day, and as it was a size 12 Vera Wang, it was sold that very day, and the bridesmaid was in charge of sending it on to the next bride while the original bride and groom flew off on their honeymoon.

It is the paperwhites in these winter posies that show up best in the low light of winter.

Colour scheming

Remember that white shows up well against a dark background, while reds and blues disappear in the low light levels at the dark time of year. Keep the flowers you choose light in colour, and you'll see them to best effect. Paperwhites, snowdrops, white hyacinths and amaryllis will all work well with low light levels.

If you're ordering especially for cutting, then the tallest variety I know of is *Galanthus elwesii* 'Big Bertha', and she's perhaps 25cm (10") tall. Prepare to support snowdrops with twigs, as, like narcissi, they can be leggy when they grow on in the warm, so a little nest of hazel twigs 'growing' out of a mossy surface can be the miniature woodland in which your snowdrops can flower. Snowdrops are by no means great show-offs of the cut-flower world, but there is something magical about their delicacy, and their honey scent is a surprise in a cold season. In flower lore, they represent something new, so for a wedding I think they're perfect.

Cutting and conditioning in winter

The techniques required to condition flowers and foliage cut in winter are slightly different from those used at other times of the year when the weather is warmer.

- ✿ Try not to cut flowers or foliage when they're frozen solid or covered in snow. Wait until the warmest part of the day before you cut anything. Cut into buckets of clean water, as usual, then, if the material is frozen, bring it in to somewhere under cover but not significantly warmer than the outside, so it doesn't defrost too quickly.
- ✿ Keep bulb flowers apart from any other material you're cutting, because they drool sap and make water cloudy while they're conditioning.
- ✿ Flowers from forced bulbs, when cut, will open more quickly than those still attached to the plant. If you want to hurry them up, cut bulbs when they're beginning to show colour, give them a little warm water, and bring them in somewhere warm. Hollow stems can be

This posy is mostly greenery, with the colour provided by just a little lungwort and a single bright splash of orange from one early ranunculus.

A long garland of entirely foraged material, including dried hydrangea heads. This makes a great table-centre runner, or can be hung over a mantlepiece or doorway.

Top: Dried hydrangea heads don't even need vases, but can be just dotted about very effectively.
Bottom left: A winter wedding idea – use dried hydrangeas and twigs only for a papery, vintage, attractive look.
Bottom right: In winter, willow reveals its true colours. If you have access to some, it makes good weaving material.

Slumbering wildlife

When bringing plant material indoors in winter, watch out for wildlife waking up in the warm. We often find shield bugs, ladybirds and even butterflies meandering sleepily about the studio table when we've brought in winter foliage and flowers for arranging. Take them back outside and tuck them away somewhere protected: I tend to put them in the log shed, where they can hide away again until the spring wakes them up at the right time.

filled with warm water, then put your thumb over the open stem end and put the whole stem in more warm water. This gets the warm water right up to the almost-flowering head.

- If you want to hold cut bulb flowers back from flowering, then, again, cut them when the colour's beginning to show on the flower heads, but don't put them in water. Lay them flat in a box and put them somewhere cool and dark until 2 or 3 days before you need them. You can keep them this way for up to a week. Then take them out of their box, cut 2cm (1") off the bottoms of the stems to reopen the cellulose drinking cells, and put the stems in water. They should rehydrate nicely and flower as normal.

Top tips for winter wedding floristry

- Don't expect to have masses of flowers. Plan to use foliage as a basis, and the flowers you can grow will be stars of light in the mix.

- If you are forcing bulbs, you may need to bring them into the house to speed up their flowering, so use pots that aren't too heavy to lift. If you're growing them in attractive pots, then you don't necessarily need to cut them, but can use the pots of flowers for table centres and focus pieces.

- Garlanding with greenery and using candlelight creates a stunning effect. But be careful that the candles don't cause a fire risk, and do check what rules your venue may have about open flames.

- You will very likely be able to find a local professional grower who can supply winter flowers to supplement your own stock, without having to use imported flowers. See Resources section for some websites listing flower growers (in the UK and USA).

- Cut flowers and foliage at the warmest time of the day, and put them to condition somewhere not too much warmer. You don't want them to defrost and go to mush, which might happen if they're really crunchy.

A WINTER WEDDING RECEPTION IN AN OLD COUNTRY PUB

This tiny winter wedding reception took place just before Christmas, in a pub with scrubbed tables and mix-and-match chairs. The ceremony was earlier that morning, and the guests then repaired to this lovely old place for gastronomic delights rounded off with sloe gin.

We ordered the flowers from a grower with glasshouses from which they supply throughout winter, and we foraged the greenery. There were only 20 guests, and the flowers really were a central part of the whole occasion. The day was dark, but the white flowers and lots of candlelight and glass gave light and sparkle, and a gorgeous, intimate feel.

Some guests prefer to put their buttonholes into a (vintage) glass of water rather than wear them.

Have a vase to hand, and the bride can put her bouquet into it for the duration of the reception once she's had enough of carrying it around.

A lusher mix of greenery and paperwhites make another table centrepiece. In winter especially, don't try to be too matchy-matchy.

Each guest was given a buttonhole, tied as a little posy, as their place marker.

A wreath of bright willow stems with a hurricane lamp and a pillar candle makes an effective table centrepiece.

A celebratory welcome wreath with crab apples, Scots pine, ivy and other greenery.

A long garland to go down the table, made to match the welcome wreath - note the dried hydrangeas in the mix. You certainly don't have to use all fresh material at this time of year.

PART THREE
WEDDING FLORISTRY

A HAND-TIED POSY OR BOUQUET

Practise making hand-tied posies from the day you decide you're going to do your own wedding flowers. Like any art or craft, the more you do this, the better, and the more confident you'll be at it. Make at least one posy a week, preferably two or three (your friends and family will be delighted recipients throughout your planning and up until your wedding). Then, when it comes to the big day, you'll not only be much faster but also have a really clear idea of how much material you'll need for each of your arrangements, which will inform your cutting schedule too (see Chapter 3, page 53).

The method for making a hand-tied bouquet is the same as for a posy – it's just a matter of scale. When you're practised with making small posies, you can build up to a larger bouquet.

What you'll need

Gather together everything you need before you start. You will need:

- A good selection of well-conditioned flowers and foliage to practise with. I recommend about two-thirds flowers to one-third foliage. The foliage is useful not only because it frames each different flower very nicely, and gives the bouquet a proper garden look, but also because the stems are often stronger than those of cut flowers (especially annuals or heavy-headed roses), and so can work as a kind of scaffolding to help hold up either delicate or heavy heads.
- For a pretty generous jam-jar posy you'll need a minimum of 20 stems.
- For a bride's bouquet you'll need perhaps 50 stems. Practice will inform how many

Practise making lots of posies well before the wedding, and when the time comes you'll be confident about how much time and material you'll need.

Keep the ingredients for your posy in water for as long as possible. Cut flowers won't like being laid on a table, out of water, while you choose what you need one stem at a time.

Have clean jugs, jars and raffia to hand, as well as a pair of carbon-bladed florist's scissors.

stems you need per arrangement for your wedding scheme.

- Perhaps one, three, five or seven 'accent' flowers (see right). The number depends on the size of the posy and the size of the accent flowers. Use odd numbers of accent flowers so that you never inadvertently create straight lines, squares or rectangles in your floristry: you're making wedding flowers, not planting up a roundabout with municipal bedding!
- Jars, jugs or vases: clean, ready, and filled with fresh water, so that as soon as your posy is made you can put its freshly re-cut stems into water, and they can have a nice drink.
- Raffia, twine, string, ribbon – whatever you intend to tie your posy with. I prefer raffia. For a hand-tied bride's bouquet or bridesmaids' posies, I use ribbon as well as raffia.
- Carbon-bladed florist's scissors: these

are much better to use than secateurs, as they will handle delicate stems more easily.
- A mirror that you can stand back from and see the posy or bouquet you're making from any angle.

Choosing your ingredients

A good posy or bouquet has the following shapes in it:

- **A larger, accent flower** In spring this could perhaps be ranunculus; in early summer, roses or peonies. Later, you might use dahlias or sunflowers. In winter, you could make bunches of paperwhites to add into a bouquet, each bunch acting as though it were a bigger flower on its own. For a small posy, one accent flower may be plenty, framed with other stems, which will also cushion and support it so that it sits at an attractive angle in its container and can be seen nicely. Heavy-headed flowers can easily pull themselves out of their containers, so be prepared to add other material to counterbalance them.
- **A daisy shape** In early summer this could be a real wild daisy, or a feverfew. In spring it could be anemones; later in the year, cosmos.
- **Lacy filler** In early to high summer, ammi majus is perfect. Earlier in the year it could be cow parsley; later, ammi visnaga. For winter, you might use a flowering viburnum such as *Viburnum tinus* 'Eve Price'.

This bouquet has alchemilla and acid-green physo-carpus as greenery, to split the flowers up and give them dancing space.

Wild scabious bouncing tall in a bouquet. This one is field scabious, which will have been feeding the butter-flies in the field until you cut it.

- **Spikes of delicate flowers** These will give the bouquet life and movement. In early summer, it might be foxgloves or delphiniums (use the heavy-headed leading flower heads for large arrange-ments; the more delicate side shoots in bouquets). Earlier in the year, perhaps common bistort or aquilegia. Later, you might use larkspur or bells of Ireland. In winter you could use bright stems of dogwood or willow.
- **Greenery** This will frame your flowers and gives a bouquet depth of field – a herbaceous-border look rather than a municipal-planting look. Look for greenery with tendrils, which can curl out from the side: clematis, sweet peas, ivy, jasmine . . .
- **Wildflowers** A dot of wildflower gives any bouquet a touch of magic. In spring there are cowslips and bluebells; in summer, it could be ox-eye daisies or buttercups; later, wild scabious . . . Winter brings old man's beard and berries like the wild spindle to give a bouquet a wild look.

Keeping your ingredients in water

Many florists take the flowers and foliage they're going to use and lay it all out on their counter, so they can pick flowers up easily stem by stem. But I recommend that you keep your material in its bucket and pull out stems one at a time to add to your hand-tied posy. This way you won't give your flower stems time to dry out, or put your flower heads under any stress while you arrange them. Your material has not been treated with lots of preserving chemicals, and it will much prefer to be kept in water.

These hand-tied bouquets can take a while to make, especially if they're your bride's or bridesmaids' bouquets. (I am a very experienced florist and typically it will take me over an hour to create a bride's bouquet, while a little, relatively easy jam-jar posy will still probably take me 10 minutes or so.)

Since you're going to keep your cut flowers in their buckets and only take them out one at a time, it's really worth stripping the stems of any side shoots and foliage that you won't need, before you put them in the water to condition: this way, when you pull flowers out one stem at a time, they won't pull all the others out with them.

How to make your posy or bouquet

🌹 Use your left hand as your 'holder' (assuming you're right handed), and position your left thumb and forefinger as a loose clasp. Keep your hand loose: you don't want to grip your stems too tightly, or you risk bruising them, and then they'll find it difficult to drink.

Use your left hand as a loose clasp and add stems at a slight angle from right to left, making a quarter turn after each time you've added a stem.

🌸 Take one flower to start with and put it in your hand clasp. I wouldn't start with one of your accent flowers – the start of your posy is unlikely to end up being the centre of it. Start with some foliage, or a lighter flower.

🌸 Add new stems at an angle from top right to bottom left across the previous stem in your hand. This is beginning to make the twist which will give you a hand tie that will stand up on its own, as in the picture on page 168. Keep your grip loose between your thumb and forefinger, so that you can add stems easily and you're not clenching your collection of stems into a hot bunch. Every time you add a stem, take your posy out of your left hand and turn it a quarter clockwise. Add stem, quarter turn, add stem, quarter turn. (At first it'll feel odd, and as though the angle isn't working, but keep going!) Never mind if the stems are all different lengths hanging down: you'll cut these off evenly at the end of the process. Look instead at the posy as you make it.

🌸 Dot different flowers and foliage in to the mix as you go along. The reason you make a quarter turn every time you add a stem is so that you arrange your flowers evenly around your posy, so that when it sits in a vase or jar as a table centre it can be enjoyed from all angles.

🌸 If you're making a bride's or brides-maid's bouquet, you could use a long mirror to see how the bouquet looks when being carried at waist height, and add trailing stems at the front or side,

Support delicate flowers with stronger material in your bouquet. This poppy, if properly conditioned, won't wilt during the day, but it will probably lose its petals, leaving the pretty beginnings of its seedhead. Manage your expectations of what the flowers will do for you, and you'll be happy with the results.

or taller stems at the back, if that's the look you'd like to go for (see 'Practice tips' on the next page). A mirror in the flower studio is a very useful tool.

🌸 Add your stems one at a time, placing each stem so that it sits happily with its neighbour, i.e. isn't too squashed, or falling out too loosely. Don't use all your favourites at once, or you'll end up with a posy very flower-jammed on one side and with just a thick collar of foliage. Dotting foliage among your flowers helps keeps the look light and informal – more 'fresh from the garden'.

Cut the stems evenly across when you've tied your bouquet or posy and it should stand up for you like this. I recommend you get it straight into water when you've cut the stems, so that they keep drinking and keeping the flower heads beautiful for your big day.

It also helps to support the more delicate, potentially floppy flower heads, as well as the heavier flowers, which might otherwise pull themselves out of the bouquet and spoil the shape you're making.

🌹 It's sometimes difficult to get a real idea of how a posy is looking when seen only from above, so in our studio we have a mirror so that we can stand back with a bouquet or posy in our hands and see how it looks from any

distance. This way we can spy any gaps that have appeared, or bald patches, or flat sides – though if you give your posy a quarter turn every time you add a stem, this shouldn't happen.

🌹 When your posy's big enough for you, tie it tight. (You may need somebody to help the first time you do this, as you'll be nervous about putting it down and won't have the confidence to manage raffia, bouquet, knotting, etc. with just your own two hands.) I really recommend a doubled-up length of raffia for tying: raffia holds well, doesn't bruise the stems, and makes a good double knot without the raffia slipping. If you plan to use ribbon to tie your bouquet, tie it first with raffia and then cover the raffia with ribbon.

🌹 Cut the stems evenly across at the bottom, so that it looks tidy, and put your creation straight into water. Et voilà! Your posy or bouquet is made.

Practice tips

Weekly practice will really help a lot in giving you confidence. Posy-making can appear deceptively simple when you watch someone experienced whip up a floral masterpiece in no time. If you practise, then you'll feel a similar confidence when it comes to your wedding preparation, and you won't find it stressful creating your real arrangements.

As you become more practised you might like to add collars of interesting greenery:

Put your posies straight back into water when you've made them, and find somewhere cool, out of direct sunlight, and airy, where they can spend the night before you use them. A garage, barn or cellar is ideal.

try different trailing ingredients, such as jasmine or clematis.

If you're making your bride's bouquet, and you're feeling confident, then have a go at giving a 'back' and a 'front' to your bouquet by standing with it in front of a full-length mirror so that you can see what it looks like as you create it. But remember that there is no such thing as a perfect bride's bouquet, especially when it's home-made. All happy brides are beautiful, whether their bouquets are practised confections of great artistic beauty or a fresh and simple handful gathered almost straight from the garden.

So be sensible about the time you'll have to spend on bouquets the day before the wedding. You may only have time to do your table centres, or the ceremony flowers, or perhaps you have a big team of obedient helpers and you'll have time to do all the flowers. If everything's carefully planned, then all will go well, especially if you've had lots of practice.

A BUTTONHOLE OR CORSAGE

Here we have a bud of *Rosa* 'Compassion', just beginning to open as part of the buttonhole posy.

I'm not a great fan of the buttonhole sporting a very stiff carnation, backed by a spray of feathery fern, underpinned with a clutch of crunchy-looking dry gypsophila heads. I think you, having grown all your own flowers, might prefer to make a miniature posy for your true-love's boutonnière (and for his best man, the ushers, your dad, his dad . . . corsages for your mum, his mum, granny . . . and I know I'm making

assumptions: it might very well be he making the buttonholes, not she).

The principle of making a buttonhole or corsage is the same. Traditionally, men wear buttonhole posies in their buttonholes, but modern fashions usually have them pinned to the lapel. Similar arrangements for women are pinned to outfits or to handbags, or attached to combs and worn in the hair, or to ribbons and tied round the wrist.

What you'll need

- An odd number of flowers and leaves – three, five or seven – it's up to you. More than seven and you'll be making quite a big posy to be pinned to a lapel.
- If you choose to use wire, you'll need very fine stub wire: you can buy this in large quantities (far more than you're likely to need) from a florists' sundries supplier online, or your local florist should be able to sell you a small quantity. Very fine wire can be cut with scissors, so you won't need wire clippers.
- Carbon-bladed florist's scissors.
- Raffia or string to tie.
- Ribbon if you'd like, for a final flourish.

- Pearl-headed pins – as many as you have buttonholes, or, for heavy button-holes, perhaps two pins for each.
- Stemtex – stretchy self-adhesive tape, which you can use to bind buttonhole stems to make them tidy. Personally, I usually prefer to see the stems. It depends on the wedding and your preference: you are your own florist.

Choosing your ingredients

You'll need to remember to put aside the ingredients for buttonholes while you do the rest of your floristry. Ideal buttonhole material can always be found in side shoots, broken heads, little extras which might otherwise be composted. Keep some jars full of clean water to hand so that you can pop these little stems in them as you work, and you'll have plenty of material at the end to make a lovely mix of miniature posies that will work as buttonholes.

If you do want to have a feature flower, so that your buttonholes and corsages all have a certain look, then you'll need to reserve those flowers for the purpose. I like to keep rosebuds for this, rather than fully open roses. It's amazing how the buds open through the day (encouraged by the warmth of the person they're pinned to), and they're less likely to wilt than open roses. Though with good conditioning and careful tying, right up under the neck of the flowers when you make the button-holes, you shouldn't suffer any wilting flowers at all.

Flowers that make good buttonhole material

The kinds of flowers that will work well in buttonholes change throughout the year, but the factors that make them good can always be found in the cut-flower patch.

- Use flowers with thin, but strong, stems: tulips, roses, pompon dahlias, autumn chrysanthemums.
- By all means use flowers with weaker stems, but support them with stronger stems so that their heads don't flop.
- Seedheads make good support material: poppies and scabious are great.
- A tall, twiggy leaf makes a good background: rosemary is excellent all year round.
- Use flowers that aren't fully open: they'll open through the day against the warmth of the person wearing them.

Can I use sweet peas?

Sweet peas do work in buttonholes, but they need support. Use stems with flowers that aren't quite out yet (they'll come out during the day). If there are too many flowers on the stem, pull off those below the top inch or two of the stem.

How to make your buttonhole

- Choose perhaps five or seven short stems. You could use, say, a rosebud, a sweet pea, a sprig of rosemary, a little scabious head, a nigella seedhead, a leaf of cineraria and a poppy seedhead. Seedheads are great because they're not going to wilt, and are generally on good, strong stems.
- Take your main flower – perhaps the biggest and strongest-stemmed flower of your mix: the rosebud, say – and hold it between thumb and forefinger.

Ingredients conditioning before being turned into bouquet and buttonholes.

Add the other stems you're using around it, crossing each stem over the last from right to left and then making a quarter turn of the posy before adding the next stem (see page 167). This may feel over-fussy when you're making a posy this small, but this method keeps the flower heads tight with each other, and the stems very tidy and as tight with one another as they can be.

- For a simple buttonhole posy, you *might* (you might prefer not to) wire your main flower (see opposite). This will make the central flower very strong, helping to support the other flowers in the mix.
- Your main flower should be roughly in the middle of the mix. Use the seedheads and strong stems at what will be the front of the buttonhole, to help support the arrangement, and anything softer or less sturdy at the back. The sweet pea, for example, can be draped over the stronger rosebud to keep the flowers upright.
- Arrange the tall leaf you've chosen, and any other uprights, like the sprig of rosemary or a poppy seedhead, at the back: they'll lie flat against the clothing the buttonhole will be pinned to. (You can see that floristry is like making miniature herbaceous borders.)
- So now you should have: a main flower in the middle, surrounded on the front by supporting material and framed behind by a leaf, which will lie flat against the shirt or jacket of the wearer. All will be arranged with a tight spiral of stems, which will hold the teeny buttonhole posy in place.

When you've made your buttonhole posy, put it in water overnight to drink up as much as it possibly can. It'll last much better this way than if kept cool in a fridge on a tray, which some people advocate.

🌹 Take whatever you're going to use to tie your buttonholes, and fold a length in two. I recommend raffia, as it has a good grip and doesn't make too chunky a binding. Keeping a length of perhaps 15cm (6") down the stem of your posy (so that you have an end to tie with), start binding from tight up under the flower heads of your posy. This is important because the binding is also going to help support the arrangement you've made. Bind down the stems for perhaps 4cm (1½"). Then take the end you held down the stem and use it to tie a double knot. You can cut the spare raffia close to the knot, or make a bow, or cover the whole stem length with Stemtex, or

re-bind with a twist of ribbon over the top of the raffia.

I recommend you use something like a takeaway delivery carton to store your buttonholes when they're made. Make a grid across the top using tape, with the right number of sections for the number of buttonholes you have. Fill the carton with water, then pop a buttonhole into each section, where it can have a nice drink overnight. Pop a pin into the back of the buttonhole at this stage as well, so that you won't have to remember pins the next day, when things might be getting a bit hectic.

When you take buttonholes out of water, give them a good squeeze with a towel (real towels absorb water better than paper and leave no soggy bits behind). Buttonholes should last nicely through the day. You might, if you have time, if your fingers aren't too tired, and you think of it, make a second buttonhole for the groom, in case some of his friends have hugged him overenthusiastically before the photographs are taken.

Wiring

Of course you can wire flowers, if you want to. But for these little posies, I don't think you really need to. Your time is probably short and you won't be practised – so you might prefer to keep things simple. If you're not using wire, the trick is to keep the flower heads tight in with

Push the very fine stub wire up through the head of
your flower.

To wire a flower, use
very fine stub wire.

1. Push the wire up
through the centre of
the flower head then
bend it over and push
it back again through
the flower head.

2. Twist the wire around
the stem to reinforce its
strength.

one another so that they support each
other's heads, and to use stronger-
stemmed material on the outside to
support any potentially floppier flowers.
Wiring will help give extra strength – but
practise your buttonholes, and you may
become confident without it. If you do
want to use wire, here's how. If you'd like
to improve your wiring skills, though, you
might wish to attend a course or workshop to learn more.

❀ Take your flower and push the fine
   stub wire up through the head of it.
❀ Turn the wire back and pull it back
   through the flower head, taking care
   not to bruise petals, and making sure
   that the loop of the wire, when pulled
   back, doesn't show on the flower head.
   This is where you must be very delicate
   or you risk pulling the flower head off –

the wire is strong, and a flower can
suffer from being mauled by it.
❀ Now you could cut the stem of the
   flower off close to the flower head and
   use the wire to make a very fine false
   stem, which you can then bind with
   Stemtex.
❀ Alternatively, you can keep the flower
   stem, and just twist the wire around a
   short length of it (5cm/2" is plenty), as
   pictured above. If you keep the wire
   long enough, you can use it to bind the

Bind your buttonhole with something attractive like raffia, ribbon or wool, to hide any wire you have used.

You can wire any number of stems in the fashion I've described. If you cut the stems off and bind the wire 'stems' together, you'll end up with a very fine 'stem', which you can then bind with Stemtex, and which really can be tucked through the buttonhole in the lapel of a jacket – the reason buttonholes are so called. However, these days most people pin their buttonholes, and we find that our customers like the posy style we give them. How you make your buttonholes is, of course, up to you, but I've described the posy style in this chapter because I think it's prettier.

posy together when you've made it – this is how I prefer to do it.

🌸 Hide any wire you may have used by binding your buttonhole with something more attractive: I like raffia, but a little twist of ribbon or wool, or just plain garden twine, can also look good.

For these kinds of posies, I might wire just one flower – the central flower in the mix – and I would use the strength of that one stem to support the rest of the flowers in the posy. Although the wired stem is in the middle, tying the other flowers tight in against the wired stem gives the whole posy the strength you need.

BUTTONHOLE FACTS

Traditionally, buttonholes are worn by gentlemen on their left lapel, and corsages by ladies on their right-hand side. Gentlemen wear their buttonholes facing upwards, whereas, traditionally, ladies would wear them facing downwards. Why gents on the left and ladies on the right? Because when dancing in the olden days, a gentleman would put his right hand round the lady's waist, and the lady her left hand on his shoulder: on that side, the flowers risked getting squashed or tangled up with each other. And so they were worn on the other side – the side on which the lady and gent held themselves a little further away from each other.

A TABLE CENTREPIECE

I've already described how to make a hand-tied posy (see page 162), but not everybody wants posies for their wedding reception tables, so here's another idea. It doesn't involve any more material than a similar-sized hand-tied posy, it avoids the use of flower foam, and it has a light and elegant feeling but is low enough for guests to look over to talk to people on the other side of the table.

A grid system over a container offers lots of possibilities. For example, it means you can have candles standing tall in a water-based arrangement, because the tape grid can keep the candle upright. (If using candles, remember to check whether your venue has restrictions regarding open flames.) But the way we usually make our table centrepieces is with our collection of vintage trifle bowls, which are easily available from charity shops. Indeed, charity shops are really fantastic treasure troves for glass containers and vases for flowers.

Here the grid system has been used to keep a pillar candle in place in the centre of a glass bowl, which is then popped inside a boater hat to make an unusual table centrepiece at a wedding in a boat house.

What you'll need

- Suitable containers.
- Tape to make a grid. You can use ordinary Sellotape, or, for a bit more in cost, narrow Oasis tape is stronger and stickier, although it's also dark green, so will show unless you take care to hide it.
- Flowers and foliage. Because these arrangements are shallow, you can use all the side shoots from flowers and foliage, meaning you get more for every stem you cut.

Here a 1950s Constance Spry-ish vase is filled with flowers for a table centrepiece, using the grid system described below.

How to make your table centrepiece

❧ Take your glass bowl, or whatever container you'd like to arrange your flowers in, and first make a grid of tape to criss-cross over the top of the bowl. If you arrange the tape so that it doesn't actually cross the middle of the bowl, then you won't end up with a hole in the middle of the arrangement. It's useful to have a grid, so that you can keep short-stemmed flowers upright in the middle of the bowl, which will allow you to create a cushion shape to your arrangement.

❧ Next, fill the bowl with water, then add your greenery to make a base for flowers to sit on, and to cover up the grid of tape. I often find that the greenery base is so attractive that I'd quite like to leave it without any flowers. Make sure that the greenery hangs over the sides of the container, so as to cover up any tape stuck part-way down the sides.

❧ Then add the flowers. Make sure that you cut the stems long enough to reach well into the water, but short enough that they hang down from the greenery on which each flower head faces up, without having long stems lying on the bottom of the bowl. This will mean that there's no battle going on under the water line between a crowd of stems, making it easy for you to pop flowers into the mix without coming up against obstacles.

❀ Enjoy yourself with these arrangements. Having practised, you may find that a greenery cushion with just one wide-open rose, say, as the focus of the arrangement, is what you'd like. This is your floristry – there are no rules. My aim here is to inspire you to have a go, and to be creative!

❀ Remember, though, that you shouldn't get overexcited and make your table-centre arrangements too tall: you don't want to stop people talking to one another across the table . . .

1. Make a grid of tape on your chosen container. A small container like this may need only a couple of strips each way.

2. Add greenery to make a cushion for the flowers to sit on, and to cover up the grid.

3. Add the flowers, which will be supported by the greenery.

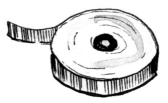

A GARLAND

Garlanding can be used to dress any number of different places. Here it's climbing a marquee pole to give some height to a wedding scheme.

Whether to adorn a long ribbon down a table centre, to hang over a mantelpiece, to swag a stairway or to make an arch over a doorway or gate, a long garland makes a stunning focal statement for a wedding.

Garlands do, however, use a fair bit of material, so I suggest you have a go at making one before you decide you must have garlanding. Perhaps just make a

length 1m (3') long, so that you can see how much material you'll need, and how much time the garlanding will take you. Making garlands is not complicated, but it is time-consuming and fiddly, and requires skill to ensure that there's a good balance in the garland, and that the weight sits right. It is for good reason that garlanding is expensive when you ask a florist to make it for you.

And garlanding really needs to be done on the day, so it's *not* a job for anyone in the immediate wedding party. But for a keen helper, and if you have enough material, then it could be fun. Anticipate a little (ahem!) stress – and, as ever, do practise.

If you plan to use a garland to arch over a church or venue door, do check in advance that there are places you can attach the garland to. Churchwardens and venue managers won't take kindly to your attempting to stick a garland to old stone if there are no hooks already there.

What you'll need

- ❀ The flowers to use in garlanding are those that won't wilt or bruise easily: well-conditioned roses, dahlias, or other larger-headed flowers with strong

Here a garland is used to dress a church pillar. Be careful with old buildings: the custodians won't thank you if you start tying up wet chunks of flower foam which will drip greenly down the ancient stone and appear to stain it. Any flower foam, or reservoir arrangements within your garlanding, must not drip or stain.

petals are good. You *can* use delicate flowers like sweet peas or cosmos, but they'll do better if there's a reservoir of water for them to drink from (more on that later).

- A good deal of sturdy greenery, which will help support the flowers as you tuck them in – ivy is good, or pittosporum; laurel if the garland is to be heavy; asparagus fern if it's to be light.
- Reel wire. You can source this online through a florist's wholesalers (it'll probably come in a pack of ten or so reels – a lifetime's supply for the amateur), or ask your local florist if they'll supply you one reel.
- String or rope, if you want to attach your garland to something to keep it hanging in smooth curves: this avoids the risk of it developing sharp corners where posies are attached together.
- Carbon-bladed florist's scissors.
- Some kind of reservoir of water for the flowers (see pages 182-3).

Choosing your flowers

Choose flowers that will survive well out of water, and often under some stress: think of the photographs you've seen of happy couples standing under a garland in full sun framing a church porch – tough conditions for flowers to do well in! Even if the flowers have a clever arrangement of water reservoirs, full sun in the heat of the day is a difficult environment for any flower to keep looking its best. Try out the material you intend to use in the weeks before the wedding, and you'll see what stands up under stress – and what doesn't. As ever, practice will make perfect.

How to make your garland

Here I describe how *we* do it (shown in Method A, opposite. A different approach is shown in Method B).

- First we make a green garland with our foliage, wired together with reel wire to make a long 'rope' of greenery.

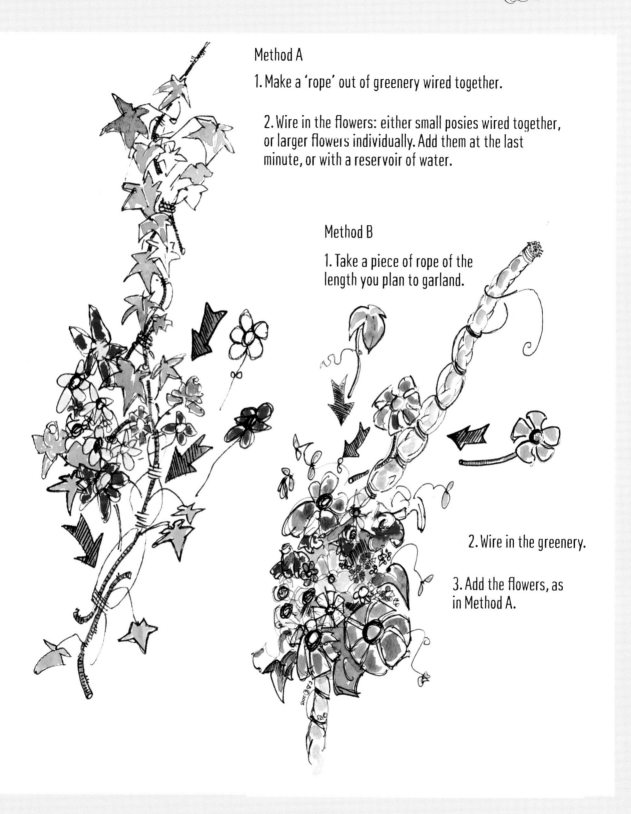

Method A

1. Make a 'rope' out of greenery wired together.

2. Wire in the flowers: either small posies wired together, or larger flowers individually. Add them at the last minute, or with a reservoir of water.

Method B

1. Take a piece of rope of the length you plan to garland.

2. Wire in the greenery.

3. Add the flowers, as in Method A.

You see how versatile garlanding can be?

* Although I don't use rope or string myself, it is useful as a measuring tool (to know how much further you've got to go). If you do use it to attach your material to, as illustrated on the previous page, it will give your swag weight and help it to hang nicely. By using reels of wire ('Method A'), we ensure that each piece of material is attached to the next – this way you can avoid there being any gaps, or the risk of the garland falling apart.
* Then we add the flowers. Basically you simply wire little posies together and then wire them to the reel wire (or rope). The posies can be as small as buttonholes (see page 172), or larger. Give some thought to how much material

you have at your disposal: large posies of course use more material. You could make all your posies first, and leave them in water to condition while you make your greenery swag.
* Alternatively, you might want to simply add one kind of flower at a time into your garland – say, large hydrangea heads, or peonies, or sunflowers. These look stunning when massed, but will need a water reservoir to keep them happy (see below).
* We then take the garland to the venue, and hang it, attach it or tie it where it's going to be installed. It's a good idea to take a bucket of spare flowers and foliage with you, so that you can fill any gaps or cover corners when the garland is hung (we call this process 'pudding'). If you're using flower foam or test tubes for your water reservoir, take spares of those as well.
* Remember to measure the length of garland you'll need, and check the length at an early stage – and remember that you'll need more material than you think!

The water reservoir

It's a good idea to give your garland flowers some sort of water reservoir, especially in the hot summer months, and there are various ways to do this. You can make little cushions of wet moss to keep the stems damp. You'll need moss pins to twist the moss on to your garland, then pop your flowers, wired so that they won't fall out, into the moss. It is also possible to buy ready-made garland nets, with flower foam inserted at regular intervals. These are easy to make garlands with, but you'll need a great deal of material to cover up the large chunks of foam.

Alternatively, you can buy little flower-foam nobbles that can be wired into the garland. These are my favourite option. My godmother, who has been a wedding florist in London for over 40 years, makes chicken-wire tubes into which she stuffs flower foam for garlands. A final option is to invest in little floristry test-tube water reservoirs. The flowers are put into the tubes, and once the garland is installed, the test tubes are tucked into the green-ery so that the tubes don't show. This was how the peonies on the giant swags on the royal barge at the Queen's Diamond Jubilee were kept fresh: each peony had its own individual phial of water.

Flowers used in garlanding without any reservoir of water will need to be extremely well conditioned, and the garland put up at the very last minute, to keep it fresh for the photographs. This is why you need careful planning and plenty of practice!

Garlanding in the making. We make it at home then transport it to the venue: it will make a terrible mess if you garland in place, so to speak. Better make the garland, then lay it flat in a car and take it to the place where it is to hang.

This is the same garland shown in the picture on the left, here used to 'crown' a marquee pole.

A FLOWER CROWN

Encourage people to wear flower crowns on the back of their heads, to keep the look light.

crown, plus greenery. The flowers have to be super-conditioned to be able to last the day. The florist will have had to finish making the rest of your floristry before starting on the flower crowns, and may need to employ an extra pair of hands especially, and somebody will have had to wire all those flowers the day before . . .

So by all means do make flower crowns, but be warned! Again and again I say: "Practise!" Practice will show you how much of everything you need. If your eyes are welling up now at the thought that you won't be able to have the crowns you've always dreamed of, don't worry. There are simpler alternatives (see box opposite). A flower crown is a stylistic commitment, which might distract you from the more important things that day.

But have a go. If everything else is ready, and you have plenty of material, and you've practised and are ready to do it, then flower crowns are certainly beautiful.

Flower crowns are fiddly to make and require a good deal of material. When your florist quotes you a surprisingly high price for your crowns, this is why. There'll be a lot of rosebuds, or dahlias, or daisies, or whatever it is you've asked for in each

What you'll need

- A lot of well-conditioned, individually wired flowers (at least 20, if you're planning to have flowers all the way round the crown).

These heavier crowns are made with a tiny sausage of flower foam, wrapped in Cling Film and wired on to the frame, so the delicate, potentially wiltier flowers have a reservoir of water to keep them fresh. This is a much heavier look, and each crown takes as much material as a bridesmaid's posy.

- 🌹 Long trails of greenery – ivy is good.
- 🌹 Carbon-bladed florist's scissors.
- 🌹 Reel wire.*
- 🌹 Stemtex.*
- 🌹 Very fine stub wire.*
- 🌹 Ribbon is useful for finishing: for hiding any problems, but also to give extra strength to the hook at the back.

*See page 180 for more about reel wire, and pages 170-1 for details of Stemtex and stub wire.

Choosing your flowers

Don't use wilty daisies or any flowers that are easily bruised. However much you've practised, you should still use flowers that don't wilt easily out of water. Well-conditioned roses, sturdy dahlias, cornflowers, nigella, astrantia, statice and pinks all make good material for flower crowns.

Alternative flower crown ideas

You can simply twist long strings of ivy into circles and wire in just a few flowers. This is a delicate and very light look.

A few single flower stems, beautifully conditioned, and perhaps wired for extra strength, can be just tucked into a simple hair up-do. This is an even lighter look, requires much less time and preparation, and is just as pretty – if not prettier. A single rose tucked into a chignon and secured with a pin will hold all day and be stunning, and won't ruin your hair-do when it falls out.

How to make your flower crown

- 🌹 First wire the flowers you're going to use, and put them to one side in water (see page 174 for how to wire). You could do this the day before. Leave enough stem length – perhaps 5cm (2") – when wiring so that a little of the flower stem can reach a water reservoir while it's waiting to be used in the crown.
- 🌹 Roughly measure the head of the person who'll wear the crown, and twist three lengths of reel wire together so they're nice and strong. The twisted wire should be long enough so that when held around the head, one end will hook into the other to join the circle.
- 🌹 Bind this with Stemtex, to cover the wire and give you a strong base upon

which to add your flowers and greenery.

- Twist a long stem of ivy around the crown shape, and you can see you're beginning to get somewhere.

- Now, one at a time, starting at one end, wire your flowers on to the crown. Start with the first flower head facing one end of the crown, and wire the flowers and foliage you've chosen on to the crown all facing the same way around the circle, or you'll be bruising flowers as you go round. This way, there'll be a pleasing regularity to the crown. Also, it'll be nicely balanced and won't fall off the wearer's head.

- Use ribbon to cover up the workings if your wire shows, or just to give a little finish to the hook at the back. I use 16mm ($^{5}/_{8}$") ribbon, because anything wider tends to clash with the flowers. You could use narrower

ribbon: a handful of different-coloured 3mm ($^{1}/_{8}$") ribbons is very pretty, making the flower crown look like the top of a mini maypole.

- A lighter crown can be made using ribbon to dance between the flowers around the crown. With fewer flowers, this takes less time to make, and can be a good idea for children, who sometimes baulk at the idea of a heavy crown on their heads. Be aware that with heavy crowns, the people who are going to wear them will need to be able to handle the weight without messing up their hair-dos.

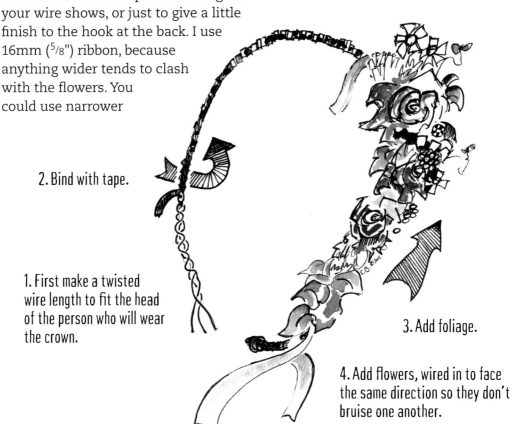

2. Bind with tape.

1. First make a twisted wire length to fit the head of the person who will wear the crown.

3. Add foliage.

4. Add flowers, wired in to face the same direction so they don't bruise one another.

FRESH PETAL CONFETTI

On the morning of the wedding, a quiet walk around the garden shaking rose petals into a basket can be a great way to just calm down and have a little time out before events get under way.

Churches and other wedding venues are often pernickety about paper confetti being chucked about to blow around all over their swept paths and green lawns – and understandably so. An increasing number of businesses are making dried-petal confetti to replace the paper version, and these make an attractive alternative. But you can go one better yourself, and make fresh petal confetti to celebrate with the happy couple.

In addition to keeping venue managers happy, fresh petal confetti has other benefits . . .

🌹 The weight of the water in the petals makes them heavier and better to throw. Dry confetti can be so light that it is literally blown away by the wind, whereas fresh petals will more likely land in the direction they're thrown.

🌹 Fresh petal confetti really can match your wedding scheme – especially if it's made out of the leftovers when you've finished doing your wedding flowers.

It is, however, something to make at the very last minute. For each day that fresh petal confetti is left to curl, the browner its edges will be, and the more bruised and creased the petals look. So make fresh petal confetti the day of the wedding, or

Rose petals are nice and heavy for a good throwing confetti mix.

Fresh petal confetti is fun to throw and biodegradable, so more popular with venues.

perhaps at most the day before, especially if you plan to use it as part of your decorations as well as for throwing.

It's important to make sure the flowers are dry before you start pulling the petals off, or you risk bruising them. If the weather's wet, you can always cut the flowers you'll use for confetti the day before you need them, and put them aside to dry off overnight.

Ingredients

Rose petals are the obvious choice: they make great confetti because they're large and therefore heavy, and easy to pull from the flower. If roses are really blown, then you can simply shake the flower heads and the petals will fall off into the basket.

Then there are lots of good flowers you can add to the mix. Look closely at the petals of the different flowers growing in your garden, to see how strong they are: how they'll stand out of water. Poppies, for example, are clearly very fragile and look as though they'd bruise in a heartbeat (which they do). Dahlias, roses, cornflowers and so on, all look, and are, stronger. As with all the ideas I suggest in this book, practise making your confetti before the big day, and you'll come up with a mix which you like and which suits you, and which will last the short time you need it to before being thrown or scattered.

The example shown in the picture opposite (bottom left) has:

- Creamy-white rose petals, for weight.
- Champagne-coloured 'Alba' California poppies, for a real bridal-satin look.
- White nigella, which has petals of unparalleled delicacy.
- Blue cornflowers – because I love them, and because pulled away from the flower head you'll see that each cornflower petal, is, in fact, a teeny single flower.
- Bupleurum, because I like a spot of green in the mix.

Good flowers to use are larkspur and cornflowers, but also bupleurum for a spot of green in the mix. Lavender or rosemary spurs make a lovely scent.

How to make your confetti

Simply pull all the petals off into a basket and mix them up a bit, as you might a pretty salad. Don't put too much in a basket at once, or you risk bruising the petals. About 5cm (2") is plenty deep enough, so you might need several baskets – which are lovely for bridesmaids or pages to carry, as an alternative to posies. If you make your fresh confetti the day before, then keep it somewhere cool and out of direct sunlight until you need it.

Be creative with confetti

You don't only have to throw confetti: you can use it to dress a table, or even a cake – scatter petals over a cloth, or make patterns with it. Or, if the flowers are edible (cornflowers and roses, for example), add them to a sparkling cocktail mix. Do be careful to make sure any flowers you plan to use in food or drink preparation really are edible! Larkspur, foxgloves and monks-hood, for example, are poisonous, and even sweet peas are mildly poisonous.

Mix the petals up as you might a pretty salad.

Blown dahlias might not last the day in a warm venue, but the petals will scatter very prettily around the tables.

AFTERWORD

Growing your own wedding flowers is supposed to be fun. The flowers you grow yourself will certainly save you a good deal of money on your wedding budget, but the idea is also to have a lovely time. Weddings are about celebration and enjoyment, and anything that adds any stress to the occasion is to be avoided. So I hope that this book has inspired you to grow your own wedding flowers, but also that it has helped you manage your expectations, enabling you to turn your dream into reality without last-minute panics or unexpected disasters.

The route to success is in the planning, in practising, in having a good team of obedient helpers and – however unromantic it may sound – in the spreadsheet!

And the sensible couple will decide how much time they really have and what they can sensibly achieve. Will you grow and arrange all the flowers? Will you find a florist to help you who'll use your flowers? Or will you keep the pressure down and let the florist do the bouquets, bridesmaids' posies and buttonholes with flowers supplied, while you grow and arrange the table centrepieces and reception flowers? This is the approach taken by many of the DIY brides who come to Common Farm Flowers. Perhaps you might grow just some of the material you need, and source supplementary stock from local growers? Will you have someone earmarked to deliver extra supplies in case you need them?

However you choose to use your own flowers for your wedding, I hope this book has left you feeling can-do and positive about the project before you. While the point of a wedding is that two people stand up and plight their troth in front of friends and family, the bonus pride when you carry a bouquet of your own beautiful, scented, bee-feeding, carbon-footprint-avoiding, flower-miles-and-chemical-free, fresh-as-they-can-be flowers down the aisle is well earned. Growing and arranging your own wedding flowers is a great achievement, and something you can remember with joy for the rest of your life. So: good luck, and happy growing.

Opposite: A celebration of colour in this mix of pot marigolds, scabious, feverfew, penstemons and more.

APPENDIX 1: PLANT NAMES

The following table gives the common and Latin names for all the plants mentioned in this book. The first column gives the name by which a plant is commonly known to gardeners: this is often an abbreviated version of the Latin name, rather than the plant's traditional common name.

Commonly known as	Latin name	Also known as	Notes*
Achillea	*Achillea* spp.	Yarrow	Be wary of contact dermatitis when cutting and using in floristry. Wear gloves and long sleeves.
Acidanthera	*Gladiolus murielae*	Abyssinian gladiolus	Very highly scented: don't use too many in arrangements or the scent may be overpowering.
Alchemilla	*Alchemilla mollis*	Lady's mantle	Be wary of contact dermatitis when cutting and using in floristry. Wear gloves and long sleeves.
Allium	*Allium* spp.	Ornamental onion	Can be smelly when cut, but the smell soon disappears and the flowers are beautiful.
Amaryllis	*Hippeastrum* spp.		Fill stems with warm water to encourage them to open.
Ammi majus	*Ammi majus*	Bullwort	Arguably the most useful cut flower for summer weddings.
Ammi visnaga	*Ammi visnaga*	Toothpick bishop's weed	Heavier-stemmed and later-flowering than ammi majus.
Amaranthus	*Amaranthus caudatus*	Love-lies-bleeding; careless	Coloured seedheads are striking in arrangements. Remove wilty leaves and use draping flower heads.
Anemone	*Anemone coronaria*		Try 'The Bride' for a weddingy look.
Apple	*Malus* spp.		You could wire the fruit to the branches to stop them falling off, if using them in autumn floristry.
Aquilegia	*Aquilegia* spp.	Columbine; granny's bonnet	
Artemisia	*Artemisia ludoviciana*	Western mugwort	
Asparagus fern	*Asparagus plumosus*		
Aster (perennial)	*Aster* spp.	Michaelmas daisy	
Astrantia	*Astrantia major*	Masterwort	Mature flowers stand well out of water, so good for buttonholes and flower crowns.
Balsam poplar	*Populus balsamifera*	Balm of Gilead	Foliage has a wonderful scent in spring.
Beech	*Fagus sylvatica*	Common beech	Foliage may need searing to make it stand well in water.
Bells of Ireland	*Moluccella laevis*	Irish bell flower	Watch out for unexpected thorns, which can take you by surprise but won't do any harm.
Bistort	*Persicaria bistorta*	Common bistort	

*'Edible' or 'poisonous' is indicated only where a plant is very edible or very poisonous. Beware using bought flowers on cakes unless you know they're not sprayed.

Commonly known as	Latin name	Also known as	Notes
Blackberry	*Rubus fruticosus*		Use when berries are not quite ripe, to avoid squishy black juice. Cut wearing gauntlets because of thorns.
Blackthorn	*Prunus spinosa*	Sloe	
Bluebell (Spanish)	*Hyacinthoides hispanica*		
Bluebell (UK native)	*Hyacinthoides non-scripta*		As with all wildflowers, only cut them if they're on your own land, or you have the owner's permission.
Bronze fennel	*Foeniculum vulgare* 'Purpureum'		Edible.
Buddleja	*Buddleja davidii*	Butterfly bush	Cut flowers when they're just beginning to open, as they go over quite quickly.
Bupleurum	*Bupleurum rotundifolium*	Hare's ear; thorow-wax	
Buttercup (meadow)	*Ranunculus acris*		Poisonous: don't use to decorate cakes.
California poppy	*Eschscholzia californica*		Brittle stems: take care when cutting.
Campanula	*Campanula medium*	Canterbury bells	
Catmint	*Nepeta grandiflora*		
Choisya	*Choisya ternata*	Mexican orange blossom	Can be smelly when freshly cut, but the smell soon goes away, leaving you very useful, glossy foliage.
Chrysanthemum (annual)	*Chrysanthemum carinatum*		Another good daisy shape to grow.
Chrysanthemum (perennial)	*Chrysanthemum* spp.		
Cineraria	*Senecio cineraria*	Silver ragwort; senecio	
Clary sage	*Salvia viridis*	Annual clary	
Clematis	*Clematis* spp.		
Comfrey	*Symphytum officinale*	Common comfrey	Use to make a plant-feeding tea.
Cornflower	*Centaurea cyanus*	Bachelor's buttons	Good also for confetti. Edible.
Cosmos	*Cosmos bipinnatus*	Mexican aster	
Cow parsley	*Anthriscus sylvestris*		You can use hairspray to stop it shedding.
Cowslip	*Primula veris*	Bedlam cowslip	One of the loveliest scents of the flowering year.
Crab apple	*Malus sylvestris*		Wire fruit to branches to prevent them falling if using in autumn floristry.
Craspedia	*Craspedia* spp.	Billy buttons	
Crocosmia	*Crocosmia* spp.	Montbretia	Lovely arching seedheads in autumn.

Commonly known as	Latin name	Also known as	Notes
Crocus	*Crocus* spp.		
Cuckoo flower	*Cardamine pratensis*	Lady's smock	Flowers fleeting, but last long enough for a wedding posy.
Daffodil	*Narcissus* spp.		In bulb catalogues, those known as 'daffodils' are generally less scented than 'narcissi'.
Dahlia	*Dahlia* spp.		
Delphinium (perennial)	*Delphinium* spp.		Poisonous: don't use to decorate cakes.
Devil's bit scabious	*Succisa pratensis*		
Dogwood	*Cornus* spp.		Bright cultivars for winter colour.
Echinacea	*Echinacea purpurea*	Purple coneflower	Pull off bruised petals when the flowers are going over, and use the thistley orange middles for interest and texture.
Elder	*Sambucus nigra*	Common elder; black elder	Tradition has it that you should ask the elder whether it minds being cut before you cut it.
Euonymus	*Euonymus japonicus*		This is the variegated euonymus.
Euphorbia	*Euphorbia* spp.	Spurge	Be wary of contact dermatitis from the caustic sap: wash your hands after cutting and arranging with it.
Euphorbia oblongata	*Euphorbia oblongata*	Balkan spurge	Be wary of contact dermatitis from the caustic sap: wash your hands after cutting and arranging with it.
Feverfew	*Tanacetum parthenium*		A few leaves in a cup of hot water will help with pre-wedding stress headaches also.
Field scabious	*Knautia arvensis*		
Forget-me-not	*Myosotis arvensis*		This is the common field forget-me-not.
Fox-and-cubs	*Pilosella aurantiaca*	Orange hawkweed	Closes up at night, so won't perform for an evening party.
Foxglove	*Digitalis* spp.		Poisonous: don't use to decorate cakes.
Grape hyacinth	*Muscari armeniacum*	Muscari	Pull stems gently rather than cut them, and you'll get longer stems.
Grey poplar	*Populus* x *canescens*		
Guelder rose	*Viburnum opulus*		
Gypsophila	*Gypsophila elegans*	Baby's breath	
Hawthorn	*Crataegus monogyna*	May; Beltane tree	Has been associated with bad luck when brought into the house. Read its history, though, and use it in wedding flowers.
Hazel	*Corylus avellana*		Lovely hazel catkins bring such promise of spring.
Helenium	*Helenium* spp.	Sneezeweed	
Hellebore	*Helleborus* spp.		Cut once the flowers are beginning to set seed, and they'll last longer in arrangements.

Commonly known as	Latin name	Also known as	Notes
Hogweed	Heracleum sphondylium	Common hogweed; cow parsnip	Be very wary of contact dermatitis when cutting and using in floristry. Wear gloves and long sleeves. Not to be confused with giant hogweed (Heracleum mantegazzianum), which causes severe skin burns.
Holly	Ilex aquifolium		
Honesty	Lunaria annua		Silvery rounds of seedheads are beautiful in winter.
Honeysuckle	Lonicera spp.		Too much flowering honeysuckle in arrangements indoors can make the scent overpowering.
Hornbeam	Carpinus betulus		
Hosta	Hosta spp.		
Hyacinth	Hyacinthus orientalis		
Hydrangea	Hydrangea spp.		The more mature flowers are less prone to wilting. (Paniculate hydrangea is Hydrangea paniculata.)
Icelandic poppy	Papaver nudicaule	Arctic poppy	
Iris (bearded)	Iris germanica		
Iris (Dutch)	Iris x hollandica		
Ivy	Fatshedera lizei	Tree ivy	
Jacob's ladder	Polemonium spp.		Lovely delicate spikes of unusual flowers.
Japanese anemone	Anemone hupehensis / Anemone x hybrida		
Jasmine	Jasminium officinale; Jasminium polyanthum		J. officinale (common jasmine) is deciduous; J. polyanthum (many-flowered jasmine) is evergreen.
Knapweed	Centaurea nigra	Common knapweed; hardheads	
Lamb's ears	Stachys byzantina		
Larkspur	Consolida spp.		Poisonous: don't use to decorate cakes.
Laurel	Prunus laurocerasus	Cherry laurel	Good as a base for large pedestals or garlanding. Tough as old boots.
Lavender	Lavandula spp.		Very calming scent in bouquets and buttonholes – good for nervous brides and grooms.
Lilac	Syringa vulgaris		Some people think lilac bad luck to bring into the house; I say absolve it and use it for the glorious scent!
Loosestrife 'Firecracker'	Lysimachia ciliata 'Firecracker'		We grow this for its foliage.
Lungwort	Pulmonaria spp.		Use in water-based arrangements in late winter. Can be wilty but will recover in water.
Maple	Acer spp.		

Commonly known as	Latin name	Also known as	Notes
Meadow cranesbill	*Geranium pratense*		Very hard to condition. I would use garden cultivars instead.
Mint	*Mentha* spp.		Edible.
Monkshood	*Aconitum napellus*		Very poisonous. If you must cut it, wear gloves. And never use to decorate a cake.
Myrtle	*Myrtus communis*	Common myrtle	Emblematic of marriage.
Narcissus	*Narcissus* spp.		
Nerine lily	*Nerine bowdenii*	Bowden Cornish lily	
Nettle	*Urtica dioica*	Stinging nettle	Use to make a plant-feeding tea.
Nigella	*Nigella damascena*	Love-in-a-mist	Seedheads as well as flowers useful in floristry. (*Nigella damascena* is the classic love-in-a-mist. Also try N. *papillosa*, with its distinctive foliage.)
Oak	*Quercus* spp.		
Old man's beard	*Clematis vitalba*	Traveller's joy	Sprayed with hairspray, this won't shed if used dry in winter wedding schemes.
Orlaya	*Orlaya grandiflora*	White laceflower	
Ornithogalum	*Ornithogalum* spp.	Star of Bethlehem	
Ox-eye daisy	*Leucanthemum vulgare*		This is the wild field daisy.
Paperwhite narcissus	*Narcissus papyraceus*		'Paperwhite narcissus' is also used loosely to mean any of the small, many-headed, highly scented narcissi commonly forced for winter.
Parsley	*Petroselinum crispum*		Edible.
Pear	*Pyrus* spp.		Wire fruit to branches to prevent them falling if using in autumn floristry.
Penstemon	*Penstemon* spp.		
Peony	*Paeonia* spp.		
Persicaria	*Persicaria* spp.		
Philadelphus	*Philadelphus* spp.	Mock orange	Classic rich, orangey scent, wonderful in floristry. Cuts well.
Phlox	*Phlox drummondii*		
Physocarpus	*Physocarpus opulifolius*	Ninebark	
Pines	*Pinus* spp.		Many different pines are useful in floristry for greenery. You can also use the pine cones.
Pineapple mint	*Mentha suaveolens* 'Variegata'		Edible.

Commonly known as	Latin name	Also known as	Notes
Pink	*Dianthus* spp.		Delicious clovey scent, reminiscent of gardens past.
Pittosporum	*Pittosporum tenuifolium*		
Pot marigold	*Calendula officinalis*	Calendula	Look for unusual colours to grow. Edible petals.
Ranunculus	*Ranunculus asiaticus*	Persian buttercup	
Red campion	*Silene dioica* (syn. *Melandrium rubrum*)	Adder's flower	
Red valerian	*Centranthus ruber*		A good wildflower. Some dislike the smell, but I've never noticed it. (The white variety is still called 'red valerian').
Rose	*Rosa* spp.		Edible petals and hips.
Rosemary	*Rosemarinus officinalis*		Use in bouquets and buttonholes to signify remembrance of loved ones no longer with us. Edible.
Rudbeckia	*Rudbeckia* spp.	Black-eyed Susan	Stands up well in buttonholes or flower crowns. ('Black-eyed Susan' is *Rudbeckia hirta*.)
Scabious	*Scabiosa* spp.		
Scarlet oak	*Quercus coccinea*		
Schizostylis	*Hesperantha coccinea*	Crimson flag lily	
Sea holly	*Eryngium* spp.		Useful also dried in winter arrangements.
Sedum	*Sedum* spp.	Stonecrop	
Smoke tree	*Cotinus coggygria*		Can be difficult to condition. Use in water-based, rather than flower-foam-based arrangements.
Snake's head fritillary	*Fritillaria meleagris*	Chequered daffodil	Pull rather than cut for longer stems.
Snowball bush	*Viburnum opulus* 'Roseum'		
Snowdrop	*Galanthus nivalis*		This is the UK native snowdrop. Pull rather than cut for longer stems.
Sorrel	*Rumex acetosa*	Common sorrel	Edible leaves early in the season.
Spindle	*Euonymus europaeus*		Gorgeous pink-and-orange berries for winter weddings.
Spiraea	*Spiraea* spp.		
Statice	*Limonium* spp.		Lovely frothy points in bouquets.
Strawberry (wild)	*Fragaria vesca*		Edible.
Sun spurge	*Euphorbia helioscopia*		As with all euphorbias, beware of the caustic sap, which can irritate skin.

Commonly known as	Latin name	Also known as	Notes
Sunflower	*Helianthus annuus*		
Sweet box	*Sarcococca* spp.	Christmas box	Beautifully scented winter flowers.
Sweet gum	*Liquidambar styraciflua*		
Sweet pea	*Lathyrus odoratus*		
Sweet rocket	*Hesperis matronalis*	Dame's violet	
Sweet William	*Dianthus barbatus*		Can also be used for spring foliage.
Tellima	*Tellima grandiflora*	Fringe cups	
Thyme	*Thymus* spp.		Edible.
Tulip	*Tulipa* spp.		
Viburnum	*Viburnum* spp.		
Wallflower	*Erysimum* spp.		
Wayfaring tree	*Viburnum lantana*		
White deadnettle	*Lamium album*	.	I love the sharp green scent of this when cut.
Wild carrot	*Daucus carota*	Queen Anne's lace	An easy wildflower to grow successionally through summer.
Willow	*Salix* spp.		
Winter-flowering honeysuckle	*Lonicera fragrantissima*		
Zinnia	*Zinnia* spp.		

APPENDIX 2: SEASON PLANNER

Use this appendix as a checker as to what's in season for your wedding, and what will suit your growing conditions. It is not a definitive list, but is intended to inspire you to do further research into what you might grow.

Plant (commonly known as)	Type	Conditions preferred*	Growing/cutting timing	Spring wedding	Early-summer wedding	High-summer wedding	Autumn wedding	Winter wedding
Achillea	Perennial	Sunny aspect, well-drained soil.	Use foliage and flowers all summer long.			●	●	
Acidanthera	Bulb	Hot and dry, full sun (not hardy).	Plant in spring for flowers in late summer / early autumn.			●	●	
Alchemilla	Perennial	Sunny aspect, good drainage.	Will give a second flush in autumn if cut back after first flowering, fed and watered.		●		●	
Allium	Bulb	Moist, well-drained soil; plenty of sunshine.	Plant bulbs in autumn for early-summer flowers.		●			
Amaranthus	Annual	Full sun, well-drained soil.	Sow mid spring for summer and autumn flowering.			●	●	
Amaryllis	Bulb	Compost with good drainage.	To encourage forced flowering in winter on good long stems, plant in a warm, dark place.					●
Ammi majus	Annual	Sunny aspect, good drainage.	Sow successionally for summer-long flowering.		●	●		
Ammi visnaga	Annual	Sunny aspect, good drainage.	Will cut from high summer to first frosts.			●	●	
Anemone	Corm (treat as bulb)	Moist soil, good drainage, plenty of sun.	Will flower late winter in a tunnel or greenhouse with warmth.	●				●
Apple	Tree	Sunny aspect, well-fed soil, good drainage.	Cut blossom in spring; use fruit in arrangements in autumn.	●			●	
Aquilegia	Perennial	Moist but well-drained soil. Happy in sun or with a little shade.	Foliage useful as well as the flowers.	●	●			
Artemisia	Perennial	Sunny aspect, good drainage.	Cut foliage all summer long.	●	●	●		

*Unless specified otherwise, all plants will do best in well-fed, relatively neutral soil.

Plant (commonly known as)	Type	Conditions preferred	Growing/cutting timing	Spring wedding	Early-summer wedding	High-summer wedding	Autumn wedding	Winter wedding
Asparagus fern	Perennial	Sheltered spot, partial shade. Probably best in a shady greenhouse.	Will cut year-round.	●	●	●	●	●
Aster (perennial)	Perennial	Moist soil. Happy in sun or partial shade (to be honest, they're just thugs).					●	
Astrantia	Perennial	Sun or partial shade.	Will cut from early summer onwards.		●	●	●	
Balsam poplar	Tree	Damp soil.	Cut in spring for lovely scent.	●				
Beech	Tree	Happy in good, well-drained soil – not happy in boggy or damp soil.	Foliage is lovely when newly opened in spring, and for rich colours in autumn.	●	●		●	
Bells of Ireland	Annual	Moist, well-drained soil in a sunny aspect.	Sow successionally for flowers through high summer into autumn.			●	●	
Bistort	Perennial	Damp, prefers partial shade. Bit of a bully.		●				
Blackberry	Perennial	Hedgerows. Another thug!					●	
Blackthorn	Shrub	Moist, well-drained soil; happy with sun or shade.	Use blossom in spring; fruit (sloes) in autumn and winter.	●			●	●
Bluebell (Spanish)	Bulb	Happy in drier conditions than the UK native bluebell, but still prefers damp, well-drained soil. Can be a bully.		●				
Bluebell (UK native)	Bulb	Dappled shade; moist, well-drained soil. Best in woodland or orchard.	Plant 'in the green' after flowering, or as bulbs in autumn, for flowering the following spring.	●				
Bronze fennel	Perennial	Well-drained soil, happy in full sun.	Use seedheads in autumn as well as flowers in summer.			●	●	

Plant (commonly known as)	Type	Conditions preferred	Growing/cutting timing	Spring wedding	Early-summer wedding	High-summer wedding	Autumn wedding	Winter wedding
Buddleja	Shrub	Any reasonable soil, happy in full sun or some shade.				●		
Bupleurum	Annual	Full sun, well-drained soil.	Sow successionally for summer-long flowering.		●	●		
Buttercup (meadow)	Perennial	Moist meadowland, loves sun, will grow in shade.		●	●			
California poppy	Annual / biennial	Poor soil, full sun.	Sow successionally for summer-long flowering.		●	●		
Campanula	Biennial	Well-drained but moist soil, happy in full sun.	Sow in early summer for flowering the following year.		●			
Catmint	Perennial	Well-drained but moist soil, full sun.	Cut back and feed after first flowering for a second flush flowering in autumn.		●		●	
Choisya	Shrub	Full sun, good drainage. Will do better with a little shelter – can get wind- and frost-bitten.	Useful for year-round foliage.	●	●	●	●	●
Chrysanthemum (annual)	Annual	Full sun, good drainage.			●	●		
Chrysanthemum (perennial)	Perennial	Full sun, well-drained soil; give them shelter against autumn weather.	Cut back hard in high summer for good late-autumn flowers.		●	●	●	
Cineraria	Annual / short-lived perennial	Well-drained soil, full sun.	An easy foliage plant to use almost year-round. Readily available in garden centres as bedding-plant seedlings in spring and autumn.	●			●	
Clary sage	Annual	Full sun, well-drained soil.	Sow successionally for summer-long flowering.		●	●		
Clematis	Climbing shrub	They like their feet in the shade and their heads in the sun.		●	●	●		
Cornflower	Annual	Full sun, good drainage.	Sow successionally for summer-long flowers.		●	●		

Plant (commonly known as)	Type	Conditions preferred	Growing/cutting timing	Spring wedding	Early-summer wedding	High-summer wedding	Autumn wedding	Winter wedding
Cosmos	Annual	Full sun, good drainage.				●	●	
Cow parsley	Perennial	Sun or partial shade, moist soil, good drainage.		●				
Cowslip	Perennial	Sun or partial shade, good drainage, moist soil. Will thrive in a meadow.	Sow in early summer for flowering the following year.	●				
Crab apple	Tree	Sun or partial shade.	Use blossom in spring; fruit in arrangements in autumn.	●			●	
Craspedia	Annual	Full sun, good drainage.				●	●	
Crocosmia	Corm (treat as bulb)	Sun or partial shade, moist soil, good drainage.	Use seedheads in autumn as well as flowers in summer.			●	●	
Crocus	Bulb	Sun or partial shade, good drainage. Mine love living in the grass in my orchard.		●				
Cuckoo flower	Perennial	Damp meadows and grassland.		●				
Daffodil	Bulb	Good drainage, moist soil, sun or partial shade.		●				
Dahlia	Tuber	Moist, well-drained, soil; well fed, full sun.	Don't plant out till all risk of frost is passed.			●	●	
Delphinium (perennial)	Perennial	Well-drained, moist soil; well fed, full sun.	Will have a second flush in autumn if cut back and fed after first flowering.		●	●	●	
Devil's bit scabious	Perennial	Damp meadowland ideal; plenty of water in a sunny flowerbed will work.	Sow in early summer for flowering the following year.			●	●	
Dogwood	Shrub	Any reasonable soil.	Use flowers in spring and early summer, foliage in autumn, bright stems in late autumn and winter.	●	●		●	●

Plant (commonly known as)	Type	Conditions preferred	Growing/cutting timing	Spring wedding	Early-summer wedding	High-summer wedding	Autumn wedding	Winter wedding
Echinacea	Perennial	Hot, dry conditions ideal. Loves sun.	Use the striking developing seedheads in autumn as well as the flowers in summer.			●	●	
Elder	Tree	Moist, well-drained soil. Loves sun but won't mind a little shade.	Foliage useful in spring and autumn, but wilty in summer.	●			●	
Euonymus	Shrub	The plant to put in a really difficult dry, shady corner.	Useful for year-round foliage.	●			●	●
Euphorbia	Perennial	Well-drained, moist soil; sun or shade.	Useful in winter for foliage (though watch out for ladybirds hibernating in the leaves), as well as for flowers early in the year.	●	●	●		●
Euphorbia oblongata	Annual	Well-drained, moist soil; sunny aspect.			●			
Feverfew	Short-lived perennial	Well-drained soil, sunny aspect.			●	●	●	
Field scabious	Perennial	Well-drained soil, sunny aspect.	Sow in early summer for flowering the following year.			●	●	
Forget-me-not	Biennial	Well-drained soil with a little moisture; good, sunny aspect.	Sow in early summer for flowering the following year.	●				
Fox-and-cubs	Perennial	Well-drained soil, sunny aspect.			●			
Foxglove	Biennial	Dappled shade or sun; well-drained, moist soil.	Will flower again from side shoots, so if you need them later in the season, cut leading flower heads to encourage further flowering.		●			
Grape hyacinth	Bulb	Well-drained, moist soil; sunny aspect.		●				
Grey poplar	Tree	Any reasonable soil, won't mind a bit of dampness.	New foliage is attractive in spring.	●				
Guelder rose	Shrub	Any reasonable soil.	Use blossom in spring; berries in autumn.		●		●	

Plant (commonly known as)	Type	Conditions preferred	Growing/cutting timing	Spring wedding	Early-summer wedding	High-summer wedding	Autumn wedding	Winter wedding
Gypsophila	Annual	Light soil, full sun.	Sow successionally for summer-long flowering.		●	●		
Hawthorn	Shrub	Any reasonable soil.	Cut blossom in early summer; use berries in autumn.		●		●	●
Hazel	Tree	Any reasonable soil, sun or part shade.	Good for winter catkins.					●
Helenium	Perennial	Well-drained soil, sunny aspect.				●	●	
Hellebore	Perennial	Well-drained soil, shade.		●				●
Hogweed	Perennial	Moist, well-drained soil; sun or light shade.	Use the seedheads as well as the flowers.		●	●	●	
Holly	Tree	Moist, well-drained soil; sun or light shade.	Great for winter berries.					●
Honesty	Biennial/ perennial	Well-drained, moist soil; sun or light shade.	Use the flowers early in the year; the seedheads from late summer onwards.	●	●		●	●
Honeysuckle	Climbing shrub	Any well-drained, moist soil; full sun or some shade.			●			
Hornbeam	Tree	Grow where soil too damp for beech trees.	Attractive foliage when newly opened and for colour in autumn.	●	●		●	
Hosta	Perennial	Cool, moist soil with good drainage; shade.	Use the leaves as gorgeous foliage.		●			
Hyacinth	Bulb	Well-drained compost.	Bring in to the warm to force for winter weddings.	●				
Hydrangea	Shrub	Well-drained, moist soil; sun or light shade.	Use the flower heads dry in winter as well as fresh from high summer onwards.			●	●	●
Icelandic poppy	Biennial	Well-drained soil, full sun.	Sow in early summer for flowering the following year.		●			
Iris (bearded)	Perennial	Well-drained soil, full sun. Plant rhizomes facing south so leaves don't shade them.			●			

Plant (commonly known as)	Type	Conditions preferred	Growing/cutting timing	Spring wedding	Early-summer wedding	High-summer wedding	Autumn wedding	Winter wedding
Iris (Dutch)	Bulb	Well-drained soil, full sun.	Plant in autumn for spring flowering the following year.	●	●			
Ivy	Perennial	Moist, well-drained soil; full sun or part shade.	Use foliage year-round (be careful not to disturb nesting birds in spring); the flowers and berries for winter weddings.	●	●	●	●	●
Jacob's ladder	Perennial	Good soil; sun or partial shade.				●		
Japanese anemone	Perennial	Moist, well-drained soil; sun or part shade.				●	●	●
Jasmine	Perennial	Well-drained soil, sun or part shade.	Use foliage year-round.	●	●	●	●	
Knapweed	Perennial	Well-drained soil, full sun.			●	●	●	
Lamb's ears	Perennial	Well-drained, moist soil; full sun.	Spring flowers and season-long foliage.			●	●	
Larkspur	Annual	Well-drained soil, full sun.	Sow successionally for a long flowering season.			●	●	
Laurel	Shrub	Any well-drained soil.	Use foliage year-round.	●	●	●	●	●
Lavender	Perennial	Well-drained soil, full sun. Shelter from late frosts.	Will flower again if cut back after first flush.			●	●	
Lilac	Shrub	Well-drained, moist soil; full sun.	Lovely flowers in spring / early summer.	●	●			
Loosestrife 'Firecracker'	Perennial	Moist, well-drained soil; full sun or partial shade. Can be a bully.	Use the dramatic foliage throughout the growing season.	●	●	●	●	
Lungwort	Perennial	Shade.		●				
Maple	Tree	Moist, well-drained soil.	Use foliage when newly opened, and for rich colours in autumn.	●	●		●	●
Mint	Perennial	Moist soil, full sun, happy also in shade.	Useful foliage from spring, flowers in high summer. Grows roots in water, so very easy to propagate.	●	●	●		

Plant (commonly known as)	Type	Conditions preferred	Growing/cutting timing	Spring wedding	Early-summer wedding	High-summer wedding	Autumn wedding	Winter wedding
Myrtle	Shrub	Moist, well-drained soil; full sun. Shelter from cold winds.	Flowers in high summer; good for foliage year-round.	●	●	●	●	●
Narcissus	Bulb	Well-drained, moist soil; sun or dappled shade.	Plant bulbs in autumn for flowering the following spring.	●				
Nerine lily	Bulb	Well-drained soil, full sun.	Plant bulbs in spring for flowering in autumn.				●	
Nigella	Annual	Hot and dry, well-drained soil.	Sow successionally for long-season flowering. Use the seedheads too.		●	●	●	
Oak	Tree	Any reasonable soil.	Use newly opened foliage early in the year, and acorns in autumn.	●	●		●	
Old man's beard	Climbing shrub	Roots in shade, flowers in sun. Good, well-drained soil. Useful but thuggish – don't plant it especially.					●	●
Orchid (many native UK species)	Perennial	Sun or partial shade. Meadows ideal. Will not tolerate any chemical intervention, e.g. field run-off of fertilizers or pesticides.	The UK native species flower in early summer.		●			
Orlaya	Annual	Full sun; moist, well-drained soil.	Sow successionally for summer-long flowering.		●	●		
Ornithogalum	Bulb	Well-drained, moist soil; sunny aspect.		●				
Ox-eye daisy	Perennial	Moist, well-drained soil; full sun.			●			
Paperwhite narcissus	Bulb	Very well-drained soil.	Will need warmth to force for winter weddings.	●				●
Parsley	Biennial	Moist, well-drained soil; full sun.	Sow in early summer for flowers the following year.		●			
Pear	Tree	Moist, well-drained soil.	Use blossom in spring; fruit in arrangements in autumn.	●			●	

Plant (commonly known as)	Type	Conditions preferred	Growing/cutting timing	Spring wedding	Early-summer wedding	High-summer wedding	Autumn wedding	Winter wedding
Penstemon	Perennial	Moist, well-drained soil; full sun.				●	●	
Peony	Perennial	Plant shallowly in moist, well-drained soil in full sun.	May take some years to settle in before flowering. Use plants you know to flower well, rather than planting especially for your wedding.		●			
Persicaria	Perennial	Moist, well-drained soil; full sun or partial shade.				●	●	
Philadelphus	Shrub	Moist, well-drained soil. Sun or partial shade.	Beautifully scented flowers in early summer.		●			
Phlox	Perennial	Moist, well-drained soil; full sun or partial shade. Protect from slugs.	'Chelsea chop' in May for more abundant flowering in late summer.			●	●	
Physocarpus	Shrub	Any reasonable soil.	Flowers late spring / early summer; great for foliage from spring to autumn.	●	●	●	●	
Pine	Tree	Moist, well-drained soil; full sun.	Use for greenery, and for cones too in autumn and winter.	●	●	●	●	●
Pineapple mint	Perennial	Moist, well-drained soil; full sun.	Useful foliage from spring, flowers in high summer. Grows roots in water, so very easy to propagate.	●	●	●		
Pink	Perennial	Dry, well-drained soil; full sun.			●	●		
Pittosporum	Shrub	Moist, well-drained soil. Protect from wind.	Great for year-round foliage.	●	●	●	●	●
Pot marigold	Annual	Well-drained soil, full sun.	Sow successionally for summer-long flowers.		●	●		
Ranunculus	Perennial	Very well-drained soil, full sun. Soak claws for several hours till they are plump before planting.	Will flower earlier in a warm greenhouse or tunnel.	●				●

Plant (commonly known as)	Type	Conditions preferred	Growing/cutting timing	Spring wedding	Early-summer wedding	High-summer wedding	Autumn wedding	Winter wedding
Red campion	Perennial	Moist, well-drained soil. Meadow conditions ideal.		●	●			
Red valerian	Perennial		Sow in autumn for flowering the following summer.		●			
Rose	Shrub	Moist, well-drained, fertile soil. Full sun or part shade.	Cut back and feed after first flowering for a second flush in autumn.		●		●	
Rosemary	Perennial	Well-drained soil, full sun.	Scented foliage useful year-round. Flowers in spring.	●	●	●	●	●
Rudbeckia	Annual	Moist, well-drained soil; full sun				●	●	
Scabious	Annual / perennial	Well-drained soil, full sun.				●	●	
Scarlet oak	Tree	Any reasonable soil, sun or woodland setting.	Use newly opened foliage early in the year, and acorns in autumn.	●	●		●	
Schizostylis	Bulb	Moist, well-drained soil; full sun.	Plant bulbs in spring for autumn flowering.				●	
Sea holly	Perennial	Well-drained soil, full sun.	Sow seed in early summer for flowers the following year. Use dried in winter.			●	●	●
Sedum	Perennial	Moist, well-drained soil; full sun.	Use foliage before flowering as well as the flowers when they are out in late summer.			●	●	
Smoke tree	Shrub	Moist, well-drained soil; full sun. Won't flourish if you crowd it in a border.	Foliage is big and lush enough to cut by high summer.			●	●	
Snake's head fritillary	Bulb	Moist, well-drained soil. Loves a meadow situation to encourage stem length.		●				
Snowball bush	Shrub	Any reasonable soil, sun or woodland setting.	Lovely flowers early in the year. Its foliage is also attractive when young, and for rusty colour in autumn.	●	●		●	

Plant (commonly known as)	Type	Conditions preferred	Growing/cutting timing	Spring wedding	Early-summer wedding	High-summer wedding	Autumn wedding	Winter wedding
Snowdrop	Bulb	Moist, well-drained soil; sun in spring, shade through summer so ground doesn't dry out.						●
Sorrel	Perennial	Moist, well-drained soil; full sun.			●			
Spindle	Shrubby tree	Any reasonable soil, sun or dappled shade.	Brilliant autumn/winter berries.				●	●
Spiraea	Shrub	Moist, well-drained soil; full sun.	Flowers in summer, though foliage can also be used through the season.		●	●		
Statice	Annual / short-lived perennial	Well-drained soil, full sun.				●		
Strawberry (wild)	Perennial	Moist, well-drained soil; sun or dappled shade.			●	●		
Sun spurge	Perennial	Well-drained soil, full sun.	Use flowers for filler in spring, foliage for filler in autumn.	●			●	
Sunflower	Annual	Well-drained soil, full sun.	Sow direct in the ground in late spring for a late-summer show.			●	●	
Sweet box	Shrub	Moist, well-drained soil; shade.	Deliciously scented flowers in winter.					●
Sweet gum	Tree	Moist, well-drained soil; sun or part shade.					●	
Sweet pea	Annual	Humus-rich, well-drained soil; sun or dappled shade.	Sow successionally for season-long flowers.		●	●	●	
Sweet rocket	Biennial	Moist, well-drained soil; sun or part shade.	Sow in early summer for flowers the following year.		●			
Sweet William	Biennial	Well-drained soil, full sun.	Sow in early summer for flowers in early summer the following year. Foliage can be used in spring.	●	●			
Tellima	Perennial	Moist, rich soil; part shade.		●				

Plant (commonly known as)	Type	Conditions preferred	Growing/cutting timing	Spring wedding	Early-summer wedding	High-summer wedding	Autumn wedding	Winter wedding
Thyme	Perennial	Well-drained soil, full sun.			●			
Tulip	Bulb	Well-drained soil, full sun.	Plant bulbs in late autumn for flowers in spring.	●				
Viburnum (winter-flowering varieties)	Shrub	Any reasonable soil, full sun or part shade.	Use for foliage and the deliciously scented flowers in winter.					●
Wallflower	Biennial	Well-drained soil, full sun.	Sow in early summer for flowers the following year.	●	●			
Wayfaring tree	Shrubby tree	Any reasonable soil, sun or part shade.	Flowers early in the year, also useful foliage and berries in autumn.	●	●		●	
White deadnettle	Perennial	Moist, well-drained soil. Hedgerows.		●	●			
Wild carrot	Annual / biennial	Moist, well-drained soil; sun or part shade.	Sow successionally for summer-long flowering.		●	●	●	
Willow	Tree	Moist soil, sun or part shade.	Use for bright, winter stems and springtime catkins (pussy willow).	●				●
Winter-flowering honeysuckle	Shrub	Well-drained soil, full sun or part shade.						●
Zinnia	Annual	Well-drained soil, full sun.	Sow successionally for long-season flowering.			●	●	

RESOURCES

The resources listed on the next few pages are UK-based. For readers in North America, a separate list is provided on pages 215-18.

UK resources

Seeds and bulbs

Don't buy seeds or bulbs from garden centres; buy direct from suppliers. The seeds/bulbs will be fresher, and will have been kept in better conditions than the generally rather hot, bright situation that is a garden centre. And remember, when choosing, to keep yourself to perhaps five or seven types of flower: ones you can grow a lot of. While it's wonderful to have many different flowers to cut from a garden, you'll need a bit of the same for each arrangement, to give your wedding flowers a consistent look. The following are a few of my favourite suppliers.

Seeds

Chiltern Seeds
Crowmarsh Battle Barns,
114 Preston Crowmarsh,
Wallingford OX10 6SL
www.chilternseeds.co.uk
Tel: +44 (0)1491 824675
A really comprehensive seed list, especially good for those who are perhaps looking for more unusual flowers. A new grower might find the list too much, but for an experienced gardener, a few hours spent trawling this Aladdin's Cave is a treat.

Easton Walled Gardens
Easton, Grantham,
Lincs NG33 5AP
www.eastonwalledgardens.co.uk
Tel: +44 (0)1476 530063
Ursula Cholmeley sells the seed she saves from the 90-something varieties of sweet peas she grows in the 'Pickery' at Easton. This is a great garden to visit if you'd like to be inspired by plants grown especially for cutting.

Emorsgate Seeds
Limes Farm, Tilney All Saints,
King's Lynn, Norfolk PE34 4RT
www.wildseed.co.uk
Tel: +44 (0)1553 829028
A good supplier of wildflower seed, Emorsgate will tell you which part of the UK the seed comes from if you're really concerned to keep strictly local.

Higgledy Garden
http://higgledygarden.com
Benjamin Ranyard has a great website, filled with easy-to-follow growing tips for new growers. His seed is good quality, the germination rate excellent, and for annuals and biennials he has a good list. (There's no telephone number – all orders online.)

Kings Seeds
Monks Farm, Coggeshall Road,
Kelvedon, Colchester, Essex CO5 9PG
www.kingsseeds.com
Tel: +44 (0)1376 570000
For sweet peas especially – they have a huge variety.

Pepperpot Nursery
www.pepperpotherbplants.co.uk
Tel: +44 (0)1483 424614
Email: info@pepperpotherbplants.co.uk
A very good mail-order herb supplier with an excellent choice of small plants and seedlings. (Contact by phone or email only – nursery not open to the public.)

Tamar Organics
Cartha Martha Farm, Rezare,
Launceston, Cornwall PL15 9NX
www.tamarorganics.co.uk
Tel: +44 (0)1579 371098
It's difficult to find organic seed for cut flowers,
but Tamar Organics have a good, if not enormous,
selection.

Bulbs

Avon Bulbs
Burnt House Farm, Mid Lambrook,
South Petherton, Somerset TA13 5HE
www.avonbulbs.co.uk
Tel: +44 (0)1460 242177
For top-quality bulbs and wonderful, interesting
variety. Constantly wins gold medals at RHS
shows year on year, for good reason.

Fentongollan Farm
St Michael Penkivel,
Truro, Cornwall TR2 4AQ
www.flowerfarm.co.uk
Tel: +44 (0)1872 520209
An old English family firm specializing in bulb
supplies.

Peter Nyssen Flower Bulbs & Plants
124 Flixton Road, Urmston,
Manchester M41 5BG
www.peternyssen.com
Tel: +44 (0)161 747 4000
Peter Nyssen have given me the best customer
service I've ever had ever, anywhere.

Roses

The two suppliers listed here are the best known
in the UK, but do check too with your local nursery,
who may not only have a very good stock but also
be a source of useful advice. If you are going to
plant roses specially for a wedding, then the best
time to put them in is the winter before, bare-root,
and they should flower in time (so long as your
wedding date is at a rose-flowering time of year).
Do check that you're buying repeat-flowering roses,

as the one-time-only-pony rose, while always
spectacular, cannot be expected to be at its best for
you at the exact time when you need the flowers.

David Austin Roses
Bowling Green Lane, Albrighton,
Wolverhampton WV7 3HB
www.davidaustinroses.co.uk
Tel: +44 (0)1902 376300

Peter Beales Roses
London Road, Attleborough,
Norwich, Norfolk NR17 1AY
www.classicroses.co.uk
Tel: +44 (0)1953 454707

Dahlias

Order dahlia tubers well in advance to be sure
of getting the varieties you want. Dahlias should
flower well, especially if they're fed regularly, in
their first year, but if they are first-season growers
don't expect more than three or four in perfect
condition from each plant for your big day. Count
how many dahlias you need for your scheme,
then you can work out how many plants.

Do remember that one dahlia can go a long way in
a bouquet or posy, and you may only need one per
table centre for good effect. The bigger the dahlia
heads, the fewer you'll have flowering on a plant
at a time, so if, say, you want a scheme made up
largely of the huge-headed 'Café au Lait' dahlia,
then you'll need more plants than if you'd like
something smaller (but still impressive), like one
of the Karma series waterlily-style dahlias.

The National Dahlia Collection
Varfell Farm, Long Rock,
Penzance, Cornwall TR20 8AQ
www.national-dahlia-collection.co.uk
Tel: +44 (0)7879 337714

Withypitts Dahlias
Turners Hill, West Sussex RH10 4SF
www.withypitts-dahlias.co.uk
Tel: +44 (0)1342 714106

Chrysanthemums

Chrysanthemums Direct
Holmes Chapel Road, Over Peover,
Knutsford, Cheshire WA16 9RA
www.chrysanthemumsdirect.co.uk
Tel: +44 (0)800 046 7443
A good selection, which can be ordered as plantlets
to be delivered in spring for potting up and flower-
ing later in the year.

Hydrangeas

Hydrangeas are another stalwart of the wedding
flowers garden that you might consider if you are
planting for the future. Order them bare-root
from Loders:

Loder Plants
Market Garden, Lower Beeding,
Horsham, West Sussex RH13 6PP
www.loder-plants.co.uk
Tel: +44 (0)1403 891412

Peonies

If you're setting up a garden that might one day
be cut for wedding flowers, then establishing a
few peony plants will ensure that your late-spring /
early-summer bride has lush, huge, scented
blooms for her bouquet. The following are two
recommended UK suppliers who have online
catalogues and will ship UK-wide.

Claire Austin Hardy Plants
White Hopton Farm, Wern Lane,
Sarn, Newtown SY16 4EN
www.claireaustin-hardyplants.co.uk
Tel: +44 (0)1686 670342

Kelways Plants
Picts Hill, Langport,
Somerset TA10 9EZ
www.kelways.co.uk
Tel: +44 (0)1458 250521

Shrubs

I don't especially recommend any particular nursery for shrubs. I think you'd do best to go to your
local plant nursery and ask. Remember, nursery-
men and women are gardeners, and gardeners
can't help sharing information, so to ask them for
help is to give them an opportunity to share
knowledge: everybody's happy!

Supplementary stock

Whether or not you're worried that you may not
have enough of your own stock for the big day, it's
a good idea to find a local supplier as a fallback
option.

The following three websites list flower growers,
as well as artisan florists who specialize in locally
grown flowers (all contactable online only):

The British Flower Collective
www.thebritishflowercollective.com

Flowers from the Farm
www.flowersfromthefarm.co.uk

The Natural Wedding Company
www.thenaturalweddingcompany.co.uk

For British-grown flowers delivered nationwide in
the UK:

Common Farm Flowers
Common Farm, Charlton Musgrove,
Somerset, BA9 8HN
www.commonfarmflowers.com
Tel: +44 (0)1963 32883
Our own company. We supply mixed buckets of
flowers for DIY weddings. Take a look at our blog
(www.commonfarmflowers.com) – a great resource
for growing tips, floristry tips, styling ideas, wedding
resources and more.

Other good suppliers of British-grown flowers are:

Flowers by Clowance
Clowance Wood Nurseries, Praze,
Camborne, Cornwall TR14 0NW
www.flowersbyclowance.co.uk
Tel: +44 (0)1209 831317

Tregothnan
Tresillian, Truro, Cornwall TR2 4AN
https://tregothnan.co.uk
Tel: +44 (0)1872 520000

Sundries and vases

Your local flower wholesaler will likely have a sundries department, but you can also find good suppliers online. Most florists' sundries suppliers will sell to anyone these days, not just the trade. The only difference is that the more you buy, the better the price you pay. I don't recommend any in particular, as they are all much of a muchness.

For the bride on a budget, eBay is a wonderful resource. Brides often use eBay not only for buying their wedding styling materials and other sundries, but also for selling them on after the big day.

Jam jars

Beware thinking that all is well because you know that Auntie Mary has a great big box of jars in her attic. She may well have those jars, but you need to get them out well in advance and check that they're the right size, not covered with labels which need to be scrubbed off, etc. If it turns out that she only has 20 jars, and you need 70 for your scheme, then do look online for sources. There are many wholesale jam-jar suppliers, and they often have an 'artisan' section where they'll supply smaller numbers of jars (say, in multiples of dozens) for artisan jam-makers and honey producers. I won't recommend any in particular because, again, they're all much of a muchness, but do check eBay as well, as another bride may be selling off a whole set (see above).

Workshops

If you're growing your own wedding flowers, you might like to spend a day or two attending a workshop, which will give you confidence in growing, cutting and perhaps arranging your creations. We hold workshops on all these subjects here at Common Farm Flowers in Somerset, and there are lots of other workshops available in other parts of the UK. See Common Farm Flowers, Flowers from the Farm and The British Flower Collective websites (details for all on page 213) for listings.

Books

For more on growing cut flowers:

The Cutting Garden: Growing and arranging garden Flowers
Sarah Raven
Frances Lincoln (1996; paperback 2013)
Sarah Raven has been enormously inspirational in encouraging people to grow flowers for cutting. I'm not sure that without her subliminal influence I would have ever thought of starting Common Farm Flowers. There are probably a great many more people growing cut flowers around the world thanks to her. Her book is a classic.

The Flower Farmer's Year: How to grow cut flowers for pleasure and profit
Georgie Newbery
Green Books (2014)
This book is for novice as well as serious growers, with a great deal of useful and practical advice on how to start a cut-flower patch and soon have it flourishing.

For wedding styling:

Paula Pryke Wedding Flowers: Exceptional floral design for exceptional occasions
Paula Pryke
Jacqui Small LLP (2015)
Ms Pryke is an internationally renowned floral designer, and her book is useful for technical detail and showing the mechanics of creating floral designs.

Vintage Wedding Flowers: Bouquets, button holes, table settings
Vic Brotherson
Kyle Books (2014)
Ms Brotherson runs the enormously successful flower shop Scarlet & Violet in London, and is perhaps the best-known stylist in the UK using a wild and naturally grown look. This book is full of lovely inspirational photographs.

North American resources*

This section is contributed by **Debra Prinzing**, an award-winning author, speaker and leading advocate for American-grown flowers. She is the creator of **Slowflowers.com**, a free online directory that helps consumers find florists, designers and farms supplying American-grown flowers. Debra's book *Slow Flowers: Four seasons of locally grown bouquets from the garden, meadow and farm* (St. Lynn's Press, 2013) received a Silver Award from the Garden Writers Association in 2014. Her *Slow Flowers Podcast with Debra Prinzing* is available for free download on iTunes or at debraprinzing.com. Note: All addresses given here are based in the U.S., unless otherwise stated.

Seeds and bulbs

Here are some of my favorite sources of seeds and bulbs for the cutting garden. These retailers supply in quantities you would expect for the residential garden, and some will supply in bulk upon request.

Seeds

Baker Creek Heirloom Seed Co.
2278 Baker Creek Rd., Mansfield, MO 65704
www.rareseeds.com
Tel: +1 417 9248917
The largest selection of rare, heirloom varieties in the U.S. All its seed is non-hybrid, non-GMO, non-treated and non-patented, sourced from a network of about 150 small farmers, gardeners and growers.

Botanical Interests
660 Compton St., Broomfield, CO 80020
www.botanicalinterests.com
Tel: +1 877 8214340
A favorite among gardeners who value high-quality, heirloom and native varieties. You'll also find USDA Certified Organic, edible and native flowers.

Johnny's Selected Seeds
955 Benton Ave., Winslow, ME 04901
www.johnnyseeds.com
Tel: +1 877 5646697
The offerings from this employee-owned company are excellent, much sought-after by DIY flower growers and specialty cut-flower farmers alike. U.S., Canadian and international shipping options.

Renee's Garden Seeds
6060 Graham Hill Rd., Felton, CA 95018
www.reneesgarden.com
Tel: +1 888 8807228
Seeds selected for easy culture and exceptional performance for the home garden, with exciting and unusual choices of time-tested heirlooms, certified organic seeds and the best international hybrids.

Wildflower Farm
10195 Hwy. 12 W, R.R.#2, Coldwater, ON L0K 1E0 Canada
www.wildflowerfarm.com
Tel: +1 866 4769453
Established supplier of organically grown, non-GMO, native North American wildflower seeds, native grasses and wildflower seed mixes.

Bulbs

Brent and Becky's Bulbs
7900 Daffodil Lane, Gloucester, VA 23061
https://brentandbeckysbulbs.com
Tel: +1 877 6612852
A comprehensive source for unique, healthy and robust bulbs (they also sell companion plants).

Eco Tulips LLC
3320 Lillards Ford Rd., Brightwood, VA 22715
www.ecotulips.com
Tel: +1 434 2426369
EcoTulips is the only supplier of certified organic tulip bulbs in the U.S.

Old House Gardens
536 Third St., Ann Arbor, MI 48103
www.oldhousegardens.com
Tel: +1 734 9951486
Known as the U.S. source for heirloom flower bulbs. The catalogs give historical details for each variety.

*A more detailed version of this section is available at www.greenbooks.co.uk/grow-own-wedding-usa

Roses

In addition to the following reliable mail-order sources, independent garden centers are often excellent sources for potted rose shrubs and bare-root roses.

Antique Rose Emporium
9300 Lueckemeyer Rd., Brenham, TX 77833
www.antiqueroseemporium.com
Tel: +1 800 4410002
A nursery source for pioneer and old roses, the Antique Rose Emporium sells and ships fragrant, own-root roses throughout the continental US.

David Austin Roses
15059 State Hwy. 64 W, Tyler, TX 75704
www.davidaustinroses.com/american
Tel: +1 800 3288893
All roses sold in the U.S. are grown in the U.S. Roses are supplied as premium bare-root, grafted onto Dr. Huey rootstock.

Regan Nursery
4268 Decoto Rd., Fremont, CA 94555
www.regannursery.com
Tel: +1 800 2494680
The largest online selection of Grade #1 roses, from producers all over the U.S. and Canada.

Dahlias

Corralitos Gardens
295 Alitos Dr., Corralitos, CA 95076
www.cgdahlias.com
Tel: +1 831 5960323
A mail-order business specializing in around 400 varieties of dahlias, sold as rooted cuttings rather than tubers.

Dan's Dahlias
994 S Bank Rd., Oakville, WA 98568
http://shop.dansdahlias.com
Tel: +1 360 4822406
Dan's Dahlias grows and sells more than 300 varieties of high-quality dahlia tubers.

Swan Island Dahlias
995 NW 22nd Ave., Canby, OR 97013
www.dahlias.com
Tel: +1 503 2667711
Swan Island is the largest dahlia grower in the U.S. From mid July to September, you can order cut dahlias by mail to addresses in the continental U.S.

Peonies

Adelman Peony Gardens LLC
5690 Brooklake Rd. NE, Salem, OR 97305
http://peonyparadise.com
Tel: +1 503 3936185
Adelman features nearly 250 peony varieties, including Itoh and tree peonies, as well as a custom peony fertilizer.

Peony's Envy
34 Autumn Hill Dr., Bernardsville, NJ 07924
www.peonysenvy.com
Tel: +1 908 5783032
A nursery and display garden, with one of the most extensive collections of tree, herbaceous and intersectional peonies in the Northeast.

Supplementary stock

Wholesale flower markets open to the public

Few large wholesaler flower centers make it easy to purchase flowers without a resale license, but some of the best you can visit are listed here. Note: "Country of Origin" labeling is rare, so be sure to ask vendors to disclose the source their flowers. Don't assume that all of the product is locally grown or American-grown.

Los Angeles Flower District
766 Wall St., Los Angeles, CA 90014
www.laflowerdistrict.com
Tel: +1 213 6273696
The Flower District of Downtown Los Angeles is a six-block floral marketplace, consisting of nearly 200 wholesale flower dealers operating under three distinct vendor groups. The public is welcome to shop here during restricted hours for a nominal fee per visit (see the website's "Hours–Regular" tab).

San Francisco Flower Mart
640 Brannan St., San Francisco, CA 94107
www.sfflowermart.com
Tel: +1 415 3927944
Named "the best in the country" by *Martha Stewart Living* magazine, this market has more than 50 vendors, both California flower farmers and importers from other markets. Open to the public from 10am to 3pm, Monday through Saturday.

Seattle Wholesale Growers Market
5840 Airport Way S, Suite 201, Seattle, WA 98108
http://seattlewholesalegrowersmarket.com
Tel: +1 206 8381523
A farmer-owned cooperative providing cut flowers, greens and ornamentals from 14 Washington, Oregon and Alaska flower farms. Open to the public from 10am to noon, Fridays.

West 28th St. New York Flower District
Located mostly between 6th and 7th Streets, New York, NY
There is no umbrella organization that oversees the many small and large floral businesses located in Manhattan's Flower District, but the intrepid DIY floral designer can buy direct from many of the wholesale houses. Always ask about the origin of the flowers – assume that most are imported, especially the roses.

Online sources

Association of Specialty Cut Flower Growers
www.ascfg.org
A membership association for commercial cut-flower growers. You can search the online database of members who sell direct to the public.

Certified American Grown
www.americangrownflowers.org
A farmer-driven program that verifies the origin and assembly of flowers that carry its label. Many U.S. floral wholesalers also sell Certified American Grown flowers.

Slowflowers
http://slowflowers.com
With nearly 600 vendors in all 50 states, Slowflowers.com is a directory of American-grown flowers and the farms and florists who specialize in using home-grown flowers. Search by zip code to find regional sources, or by "National Shipping" to find farms that will ship their just-picked blooms to you.

Floral design supplies

Most flower wholesalers offer vases and floral supplies, but you can also find good suppliers online. For the bride on a budget, eBay.com and Etsy.com are wonderful resources, especially for vintage goods.

Vases and accessories

The Arranger's Market
www.thearrangersmarket.com
Tel: +1 804 3081908
A mail-order resource for easy-to-use but hard-to-find containers, vases and vessels.

Dorothy Biddle Service
www.dorothybiddle.com
Tel: +1 570 2263239
A national mail-order resource for flower arranging, gardening and houseplant supplies and accessories. This is the only U.S. manufacturer of flower frogs – pin holders (kenzans) and hairpin holders.

Jamali Floral & Garden Supplies
149 W 28th St., New York, NY 10001
www.jamaligarden.com
Tel: +1 201 8691333
Jamali's online store is a valuable site for DIY brides, with an extensive container and vase collection. Visiting in person is a plus.

Mason jars

The ubiquitous Mason or Ball jar is an American-made glass canning jar that is an affordable vase for garden weddings. Ball's "Heritage Collection" offers colors from the past reissued for today, including teal-blue, green and amethyst, available in 6-pint or 6-quart packs. Clear glass Ball jars come in even more sizes.
See www.freshpreservingstore.com

Workshops

The "Floral Workshops and Classes" category on Slowflowers.com allows you to search for hands-on design education in your community. Here are some of the most accessible workshop venues:

Filoli
86 Cañada Rd., Woodside, CA 94062
www.filoli.org
Tel: +1 650 3648300
The adult education department of Filoli offers numerous floral design workshops and a floral design certificate program.

Flirty Fleurs
http://flirtyfleurs.com
Florist and floral design blogger Alicia Schwede offers professional-level workshops at several locations across the country. Most are held in or around Seattle, Washington, where she is based.

FlowerSchool New York
213 W 14th St., New York, NY 10011
www.flowerschoolny.com
Tel.: +1 212 6618074
Perhaps the most extensive U.S. center for floral design education geared to both professionals and non-professionals.

Flower Duet
2675 Skypark Drive, Suite 205, Torrance, CA 90505
Tel: +1 310 7924968
http://flowerduet.com
Based just south of Los Angeles, Flower Duet offers workshops on bouquets, centerpieces and personal flowers for DIY floral designers, as well as guided shopping tours of the Los Angeles Flower District.

More inspiring resources

Field to Vase
http://fieldtovase.com
The blog of Farmgirl Flowers, a successful online floral service that is committed to using only American-grown flowers.

Floret Flower Farm
www.floretflowers.com

Floret's blog is full of flower-growing inspiration and floral design tutorials.

Books

For more on growing cut flowers:

Cool Flowers: How to grow and enjoy long-blooming hardy annual flowers using cool weather techniques
Lisa Mason Ziegler
St. Lynn's Press (2014)
A commercial cut-flower farmer shares her secrets to growing cool-season floral crops.

The Easy Cut-Flower Garden
Lisa Mason Ziegler
The Gardener's Workshop (2011)
A flower farmer's guide to growing a three-by-ten-foot cutting garden.

The Flower Farmer: An organic grower's guide to raising and selling cut flowers
Lynn Byczynski
Chelsea Green (1997; second ed. 2008)
Considered the essential guide for aspiring cut-flower farmers.

Taming Wildflowers: Bringing the beauty and splendor of nature's blooms into your own backyard
Miriam Goldberger
St. Lynn's Press (2014)
The ultimate DIY book on wildflower gardening, including a primer on growing wildflowers for your floral arrangements and wedding bouquets.

For more on wedding floral design:

Bella Bouquets
Alicia Schwede
Flirty Fleurs (2011)
Floral designer, instructor and blogger Alicia Schwede showcases vibrant full-color photographs of over 100 stylish wedding bouquets.

Fresh from the Field Wedding Flowers
Lynn Byczynski and Erin Benzakein
Fairplain Publications (2014)
A complete guide to using local flowers for weddings, created for the eco-conscious couple.

INDEX

Page numbers in **bold** indicate the main source of information on a plant. Page numbers in *italic* refer to captions and illustrations.

Also by Green Books

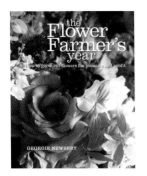

The Flower Farmer's Year:
How to grow cut flowers for pleasure and profit
Georgie Newbery

Grow your own cut flowers and you can fill your house with the gorgeous colours and heavenly scents of your favourite blooms, knowing that they haven't travelled thousands of miles – and you can make money while you do it!

Combining boundless passion with down-to-earth guidance and practical advice, Georgie Newbery draws on her own experiences as an artisan flower farmer and florist as she takes you through everything you need to grow, cut, arrange and sell your own flowers.

The Garden Awakening: Designs to nurture our land and ourselves
Mary Reynolds

The Garden Awakening is a garden design book with a difference. Drawing inspiration from long-forgotten Irish ways of working with land, Mary Reynolds re-imagines gardens for the times we live in. Under Mary's gentle guidance you can awaken your garden, nurturing the land to become a beautiful vibrant space, with garden designs that are in harmony with nature. Whether you want to bring the energy and atmosphere of wild places into your own garden, or are interested in permaculture and forest gardening, this book will guide you in embracing your garden as part of your family. Once you read this book, you will never look at your garden in the same way again.

Creating a Forest Garden: Working with nature to grow edible crops
Martin Crawford

Forest gardening is a novel way of growing edible crops – with nature doing most of the work for you. Unlike in a conventional garden, there is little need for digging, weeding or pest control. Whether you just want to plant a small area in your garden or develop a larger plot, this book tells you everything you need to know. It gives detailed advice on planning, design, planting and maintenance, and includes a directory of over 500 plants: from trees to herbaceous perennials; root crops to climbers.

As well as more familiar plants you can grow your own chokeberries, goji berries, yams, heartnuts, bamboo shoots and buffalo currants – while creating a beautiful space that has great environmental benefits.